GETTING BY
IN
CHINESE

**A quick beginner's course for
tourists and businesspeople**

by John S. Montanaro

BARRON'S
New York/London/Toronto/Sydney

Paper Edition
International Standard Book No. 0-8120-2665-9

PRINTED IN THE UNITED STATES OF AMERICA

123   550   987654

Contents

The course . . . and how to use it

Getting by in Chinese is a course for anyone planning to visit a Chinese-speaking area. It provides, in tape and book format, a basic 'survival' kit for you to use in some of the situations typical of a visit abroad.

'Getting by' in Chinese means
- managing to keep your head above water
- having a chance to make yourself understood
- listening for clues so that you can understand more
- knowing how to look up what you don't understand
- getting more fun out of your trip.

Each section of the course
- concentrates on the essential language you'll need to say and understand to cope with a particular situation — getting something to eat and drink, getting a room, getting directions, and, most important, getting to meet and talk with Chinese people . . .
- includes real-life conversations, especially recorded by native Chinese, to let you hear genuine, everyday Chinese right from the start
- gives you many opportunities to repeat and practice new words and expressions aloud in the pauses on the tape, and exercises to help you to work out for yourself how to 'get by.'

The book includes
- the texts of the conversations heard on the tapes
- a summary of what you'll need to say and listen for
- brief language notes
- tips about traveling in China
- self-checking exercises for you to do for each section

□ some extra language notes, a section on numbers, days of the week and months of the year, a list of useful addresses, the answers to the exercises and a Chinese-English/English-Chinese basic word list — a sort of 'survival' dictionary — at the end of the book.

To get the most from this course

When you listen to the tape, take every opportunity to repeat aloud what you hear, and concentrate on listening intently. The pauses on the tape are timed for you to answer fairly promptly, but they also allow a little time for thought. If the pauses seem too short at first, simply stop your tape machine and answer. Study with a Chinese friend if possible, and read the conversations aloud to check your pronunciation. When you hear the tape, *Don't just listen.* Say the expressions aloud. You must repeat the words and phrases as often as possible. If you *say* a phrase ten times, you have a much better chance of learning it than if you *read* it a hundred times. Work with your eyes only when you *can't* use the tape. When you can use the tape, *listen* and *repeat* — *listen* and *repeat*, glancing at the book only when necessary.

Do read the written material, especially the language notes, and do the exercises, looking up any words or phrases you don't know in the word list.

If you have the time, repeat each section. Go over it again and again. Listen closely; repeat constantly.

If you have had experience in learning another foreign language, it will help. But if not, don't worry. These materials are designed to 'get you by' in Chinese.

The Chinese you will learn

China is a continent as well as a country. For that reason and many others as well, different varieties of spoken Chinese exist in many parts of the country. The language you will learn in this course is based on the official language of the People's Republic of China. Fully more than three-quarters of China's billion people speak this standard language, often called Mandarin in the West. Since 1949 the government of China has encouraged the spread of Mandarin throughout the country. The words, phrases and structures you will learn in this course will be understood in all major cities, hotels, and travel areas open to tourists.

Some things might come easy

Chinese, contrary to what you have probably heard, is not a difficult language *to speak*. In fact, some believe it is easier than other languages because its grammar is relatively simple, with no case endings or verb conjugations to worry about as in European languages. Chinese grammar consists primarily of *rules for word order rather than rules for word change* (inflection).

Some things will come a little harder

Of course, Chinese has a few headaches peculiar to it. For example, Chinese words are pronounced in association with one of four tones or musical pitches, so proper pronunciation takes a good deal of practice. Secondly, you will recognize virtually no words on sight. In French or Spanish, for example, perhaps as much as 25 percent of the language is composed of cognates, that is, words that are 'English look alikes.' This is not to say that there are no Chinese words already familiar to you. There are maybe a dozen or so, mostly place names like Nanking (Nán-jīng), Peking (Běi-jīng), Shanghai (Shàng-hǎi), Taiwan (Tái-wān) or names of food like chow mein (chǎo miàn) and won ton (hūn dùn). And one other of recent popularity: kung fu (gōng-fu).

On balance, Chinese is not easier or harder, just different. Like French or Spanish — or English, for that matter — learning it takes patience, practice and persistence. The rewards are great, and the payoff for your efforts is a lot of extra fun in China.

Getting the pronunciation of Chinese

Our phonetic system

Chinese words in this book are 'pronounced' for you in a phonetic transcription system now official in China called PINYIN, which uses the letters of the English alphabet to transcribe Chinese sounds. It is a necessary tool to help you learn the language and make possible rapid progress. PINYIN phonetics, now used in China to help Chinese children learn standard pronunciation, is also employed extensively on signs and posters throughout China and is being rapidly adopted by Western media, scholars and language teachers. As a visitor to China, you will be seeing PINYIN and very likely also using it there to record words and phrases you hear.

Although the PINYIN transcription system employs English letters throughout, some of the spellings may look a bit difficult, especially those involving the use of letters, such as, *x-*, *q-*, and *z*. To aid you further, we provide a supplementary transcription system in the very first section of the book. However, you must keep in mind that the key to developing good pronunciation lies in relying primarily on the taped materials. Learn the spelling system but only *after* you have practiced the sounds on tape.

What about Chinese characters?

PINYIN phonetics offer a means to record how Chinese sounds. Many of you have seen written Chinese and know it is composed of thousands of characters or stylized 'pictures' of things and ideas. The Chinese, of course, learn not only to speak their language but also to read it. To do this, they have to memorize a minimum of three thousand individual characters and many more thousands of words formed by those characters. Here is where the real difficulty of Chinese lies—in learning to read—rather than speaking the language. Because of the unique nature of Chinese as a nonalphabet language, you can learn to speak Chinese without bothering about the written script.*

Remember that the PINYIN spellings in this book are approximations of the sounds of modern Chinese. The actual sounds *are on the tape*. Make the tape your source, and use the spellings as reminders.

For ease of reading and pronunciation, we have divided Chinese words by inserting hyphens in the PINYIN transliteration. For example, **Měiguo** (United States) becomes **Měi-guo**. However, *you must remember that such hyphenated syllables must be articulated very closely together*. **Měi-guo** is *one* word, not two.

The four tones of Mandarin Chinese

As you will shortly see in the section on pronunciation, there are only a few sounds in Chinese that do not occur in English. However, each syllable in Chinese has a characteristic tone or movement of pitch. Modern Mandarin has four tones, all of which involve different levels of sound relative to one another. A difference in tone between what is otherwise the same sound often involves sharp differences in meaning. As you go through this course, keep in mind that the tone *and* the sound make up the meaning of the word. If you have the right sound but the wrong tone, it can make for misunderstanding. The wrong tone but the right sound can also lead to difficulty.

---

*But if you're interested, see the Reference section of this book for some basic information about the Chinese written language.

No exact illustration of the four tones is possible, but most books on Chinese show the tones with a graph similar to the one shown as follows. We use the syllable *ma* (*mah*) to illustrate the four tones. Note carefully the difference in meaning for the same sound with different tones. This course follows the usual practice of showing the four tones by means of four marks above the vowel: *mā* (first tone), *má* (second tone), *mǎ* (third tone) and *mà* (fourth tone). Although we mark the tone above the vowel, the tone is on the *whole* syllable, not just on the initial sound (the beginning sound, or the *m* in *mā*) or the final sound (the ending sound, the *a* in *mà*).

Although most words spoken in Chinese carry one of the four tones, some words are toneless; that is, they are pronounced without any perceptible variation in the pitch of the sound. In this course, such words appear without any tone mark. There is also a limited amount of tonal shifts where the original tone of a word changes when influenced by a following tone. In this course you will notice such tonal alteration especially with the word for 'one' (*yī*) in Chinese. Your best rule is to follow the pronunciation on the tape in all cases.

The Four Tones of Mandarin Chinese

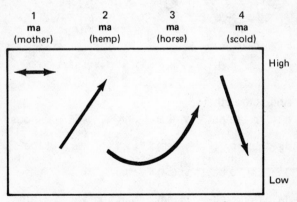

(arrows show the direction of the sound)

The preceding chart shows the four tones with the word *ma*. Note how meanings can change sharply with a change in the tone. Here's another example:

bā (bāh)
eight

bá (báh)
to pull out

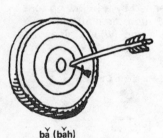

bǎ (bǎh)
target

bà (bàh)
father

And some others:

dā (dāh)	to put up	yī (ēē)	one	wū (wōo)	house
dá (dáh)	to answer	yí (ée)	to remove	wú (wú)	be without
dǎ (dǎh)	to beat	yǐ (ěe)	chair	wǔ (wǒo)	five
dà (dàh)	large	yì (èe)	hundred million	wù (wòo)	fog

Chinese, of course, is not wholly composed of one-syllable words. In fact, there are many more two-syllable words than one-syllable words. Thus, many words will combine two of the four tones. Here are the names of four places you might visit in China. They are all two-syllable words and each pair combines the four tones in varying ways:

Sū-zhōu (Sū-jōe)   combining two first tones
Nán-jīng (Náan-jīng)   combining second tone and first tone
Běi-jīng (Bǎy-jīng)   combining third tone and first tone
Shàng-hǎi (Shàang-hǎai) combining fourth tone and third tone

The basic sounds of Chinese

The basic sounds of Chinese are not hard to hear or reproduce with practice. There are only a few sounds in Chinese that do not occur in English. Unlike English, which has a rich store of individual sounds, modern Chinese has only about 400 separate sounds. Moreover, the majority of words are composed of two short syllables. This means that you will not be confronted with complicated words of several syllables.

When we think of English pronunciation, we often think in terms of vowels and consonants sort of as 'building blocks' forming multisyllable words. Modern Chinese, composed primarily of short syllables, is best approached in terms of 'beginning sounds' or initials (at the beginning of a syllable) and 'ending sounds,' or finals (those found at the end of a syllable). For example the word for *hot* (spicy hot) in Chinese is **là**, composed of the initial sound **l** and the final sound **a**. Let's now look at the initial and final sounds of some Chinese words. In the examples that follow, we will show you

1. the PINYIN spelling
2. an English description of the sound
3. an example-word in Chinese with English meaning
4. a phonetic respelling of the sound. This respelling shows pronunciation in ways familiar to you. We use this as an *aid* to the PINYIN spelling *only in this section of the course.*

Initial or beginning sounds

The following initial sounds have the same pronunciation in Chinese as in English. Pronounce them as you would English: *m*a (mah), *n*a (nah), *l*a (lah), *f*a (fah), *s*a (sah), *w*a (wah), *y*a (yah)

The initial sounds *p-*, *t-*, and *k-* are all spoken with a *strong puff of breath*; that is, they are aspirated. The presence of aspiration (or the lack of it) is an important distinguishing feature between Chinese and English.

Pinyin Symbol	Sound	Chinese Example	English Meaning	Phonetic Spelling
p-	as in *pun* (strong puff of breath)	**pén**	basin	pún
t-	as in *tongue* (strong puff of breath)	**téng**	ache	túng
k-	as in *cool* (strong puff of breath)	**kū**	cry	kōō

The initials *b-*, *d-*, *g-*, and *h-* are *not aspirated* and thus offer a real contrast to the *p-*, *t-*, *k-* sounds just introduced.

Pinyin Symbol	Sound	Chinese Example	English Meaning	Phonetic Spelling
b-	like the *p* in *spun* (no puff of breath)	**běn**	volume	bǔn
d-	like *t* in *stung* (no puff of breath)	**dēng**	lamp	dūng
g-	like *c* in *scoop* (no puff of breath)	**gù**	to hire	gòo
h-	rougher than *h* in English (no puff of breath)	**hú**	lake	hóo

This third group of initials contains some aspirated and nonaspirated sounds. Listen closely to the tape.

zh-	like the *j* in *jewel* without puff of breath	**zhù**	to reside	jòo
ch-	like *zh* above but with puff of breath	**chū**	come out	chōo
sh-	like *sh* of *shoe*	**shū**	book	shōo
r-	like the *r* in *run*	**rén**	man	wrén

The final group of initials involves the letters *z*, *q*, and *x*, all rare in English. Practice these carefully.

| z- | like the *ts* in *it's I*, without any breath | **zài** | again | dzài |

Pinyin Symbol	Sound	Chinese Example	English Meaning	Phonetic Spelling
c-	like the *ts* in *it's high* but with *strong puff of breath*	cài	vegetable	tsài
j-	like the *j* in *jeep*	jī	chicken	gēē
q-	like the *ch* in *cheep*	qī	seven	chēē
x-	between *s* in *see* and *sh* in *she*	xī	west	syēē
s-	as in *soon*, with tongue further forward	sì	four	sż

Finals or ending sounds

Let's now turn to the finals, or word-ending sounds. All finals in Chinese end either in a vowel sound or *-n* or *-ng*. Final *-n* or *-ng* are pronounced in Chinese just as they are in English, so we will concentrate our attention on the final vowel sounds. There are five final vowels (*-a*, *-o*, *-e*, *-i*, and *-u*) and several combinations of vowels (diphthongs).

(-a finals)				
a	as in *father* with the mouth wide open	mǎ	horse	mǎh
an	like the *o* in *John*	màn	be slow	màan
ang	like the *a* in *father* plus the *ng* in *song*	máng	be busy	máang
ai	as in *aisle* or *high*	mài	sell	mài (rhymes with by)

Pinyin Symbol	Sound	Chinese Example	English Meaning	Phonetic Spelling
ao	as in *how* or *sauerkraut*	**māo**	cat	māu (rhymes with cow)
ar	as in *ar* in *car*	**wár**	to play	wáar

(-o finals)

o	like the *o* in *worn*	**wǒ**	I	wǎw
ou	as in *low*	**lóu**	building	lów
ong	like the *ung* in German *jung* or like the *oo* in *book*	**lóng**	dragon	lóong

(-e finals)

e	like the *o* in *done* but after *y* like the *e* in *yet*	**dé**	obtain	dúh
		yě	also	yěah
en	like the *un* in *under*	**kěn**	be willing	kǔn
eng	like the *ung* in *lung*	**lěng**	be cold	lǔng
ei	as in *eight*	**lèi**	be tired	lày
er	like *er* in *her*	**èr**	two	ùr

(-i finals)

i	as in *machine*	**nǐ**	you	něe
in	as in *pin*	**pīn**	spell	pīn
ing	as in *sing*	**píng**	peaceful	píng

(-u finals)

u	like the *u* in *super*	**kū**	cry	kōō
ü	sound made with tongue in position of *i* (*machine*) with lips rounded	**nǚ**	female	nyěw

1 Getting to meet people

These conversations are included in the taped programs. Read them over before and after you have listened to the cassettes. Practice them aloud with a Chinese friend if possible. Look up any words you don't know in the word list at the back of the book.

Key words

Hello How do you do Good day (any time of day)	**Nǐ hǎo**	**Nín hǎo**
Good morning/afternoon/ evening	**Nǐ hǎo**	**Nín hǎo**
Good [early] morning! (before 10 a.m.)	**Zǎo!**	
How are you?	**Nǐ hǎo ma?**	
Good-bye	**Zài-jiàn**	
Please . . .	**Qǐng nǐ . . .**	
Thank you	**Xiè-xie**	

Conversations

Saying, 'Hello'

You	Nǐ hǎo./Nín hǎo.
Chinese friend	Nǐ hǎo./Nín hǎo.
Chinese friend	Bù-láng xiān-sheng, nǐ hǎo.
You	Wáng xiān-sheng, nǐ hǎo.

Saying, 'How are you?'

Nǐ hǎo ma?

And answering 'Very well, thank you, and you?'

Wǒ hěn hǎo, xiè-xie, nǐ ne?

I'm also quite well, thanks.
Wǒ yě hǎo, xiè-xie.

Good morning   Zǎo
(before 10 A.M.)

Wáng xiān-sheng, nín zǎo! *Good morning, Mr. Wang!*
Lǐ fū-ren, nín zǎo!   *Good morning, Mrs. Li!*
Gāo nǚ-shì, nín zǎo!   *Good morning, Miss Gao!*

Good-byes

Man   Zài-jiàn.
Woman   Zài-jiàn.
You   Zài-jiàn, Wáng xiān-sheng.

Making requests

When you want someone to do something for you, you
can *begin* your request with the phrase:
Qǐng nǐ . . .   *Will you please . . .*

Qǐng nǐ shuō Yīng-wén.   *Please speak English.*
Qǐng nǐ shuō Zhōng-   *Please speak Chinese.*
guo-huà.
Qǐng nǐ bāng-zhù wǒ.   *Please help me.*
Tóng-zhì, qǐng nǐ bāng-zhù *Comrade, please help me.*
wǒ.

Attracting someone's attention

Simply gesture with your hand (palm down!), and say,
Duì-bu-qǐ, duì-bu-qǐ!   *Excuse me! Excuse me!*

Finding out someone's name

You   Nín guì-xìng?
Chinese person Wǒ xìng Gāo.
You   Gāo xiān-sheng, nín hǎo.

Four Chinese surnames in the four tones

1	2	3	4
Gāo	Wáng	Mǎ	Zhào

What's your nationality?

Chinese person Nín shì nǎ-guó rén?
You   Wǒ shì Měi-guo rén.

Four nationalities in the four tones

1	2	3	4
Zhōng-guo rén	Dé-guo rén	Měi-guo rén	Fà-guo rén
Chinese	*German*	*American*	*French*

Explanations

Some basic parts of speech

Nouns

As in English, Chinese nouns name things. But in
Chinese, the noun *is not inflected* (that is, does not
change) because of number, person or quantity. So
shū (book) can mean book or *books*.

Pronouns

Pronouns substitute for nouns just as in English.

Verbs

Verbs in English change regularly because of differences in tense, person or number (I go, he goes, we go, etc.). In Chinese, one verb form usually suffices, and differences in tense are shown in other ways.

Adverbs

As in English, Chinese adverbs modify verbs. In Chinese, adverbs usually precede verbs.

Basic word order of Chinese

The basic word order of a typical Chinese sentence often closely matches English order: the subject first, followed by a verb, and then the complement or conclusion. Here are some examples drawn from the first section.

I	*am*	*very*	*well.*
Wǒ	–	hěn	hǎo.
Please	*help*	*me.*	
Qǐng nǐ	bāng-zhù	wǒ.	

Word order of questions

Asking questions in Chinese is easy. Keeping in mind the word order explained above, simple questions are formed just by adding *ma?* to statements, without a change in the word order. Here are some examples.

Are	*you*	*well?*	–
	(or *How are you?*)		
–	Nǐ	hǎo	ma?

Language notes

Some things not to worry about

Unlike other languages, Chinese does not divide words into masculine, feminine or neuter genders. What's more, practically speaking, there are no inflections, declensions, or conjugations to worry about. Remember that the basic problem in speaking Chinese is getting the *word order* right rather than learning rules about word change.

Exercises

Do these exercises after completing the program. There is a written key to all the exercises on page 72.

Fill in the gaps with appropriate Chinese words

1 It's late morning, and you meet a Chinese friend. Say, 'hello,' to him. _____

2 A Chinese friend asks you how you are (Nǐ hǎo ma?). How do you respond? _____

3 How do you say, "Hello," to the following Chinese persons?
   Mr. Wáng: _____
   Mrs. Lǐ: _____
   Miss Máo: _____

4 A Chinese asks you your nationality. What does she say? _____

5 How do you tell her that you are American? _____

6 You want to find out a person's last name. What do you say? _____

7 After finding out that the person is surnamed Wáng, say "How do you do, Mr. Wáng." _____

8 You've met a Chinese friend, Mr. Zhào, at the hotel. Respond with these conversational opportunities.

   Mr. Zhào: Bù-láng xiān-sheng, nín hǎo!
   You: _____

9 You want to attract the attention of the porter. What do you say? _____

10 You need the help of someone on the street. How do you ask for help? _____

Now thank the person. _____

And say good-bye. _____

11 Answer the question, and supply the nationality of the person illustrated:

A: Nín shì nǎ-guó-rén?
B: _____

A: Nín shì nǎ-guó rén?
B: _____

A: Nín shì nǎ-guó rén?
B: _____

A: Nín shì nǎ-guó rén?
B: _____

Worth knowing

Chinese names

Chinese surnames or family names always come first, with the given name following, in contrast to the usual Western order. Example: Wáng Dà-rén. The surname usually consists of one character and, therefore, one syllable (Gāo, Wáng, Lǐ, Zhào), whereas the given name or 'first name' is commonly of two characters but may consist of one. Given names are not merely a means of address but also have meaning, such as 'strong and capable,' typically a male name, or 'beautiful and heroic,' often a girl's name.

Names of Westerners in Chinese

When a foreign surname is 'translated' into Chinese, the most common solution is simply to transliterate the name using simple Chinese sounds unrelated to meaning. You will perhaps come across Bù-láng for Brown, Sī-mǐ-zī for Smith and Huái-tè for White. If you wish a Chinese last name, your guide can help.

Forms of address in Chinese

Except in special circumstances, foreign visitors to China will not normally address Chinese by their given name but rather use the surname with an appropriate title. When you are speaking to a Chinese, you can say

Wáng xiān-sheng	*Mr. Wang*
Lǐ fū-ren	*Mrs. Li*
Máo nǔ-shì	*Miss Mao*

When Chinese people are speaking to you, they will often use the following titles:

Mr. Brown	Bù-láng xiān-sheng
Mrs. White	Huái-tè tài-tai
Miss Smith	Sī-mǐ-zī xiǎo-jie

Visitors should be aware, however, that usage continues to vary, especially now as contacts between foreigners and Chinese broaden.

The term *tóng-zhi* or 'comrade'

When the Chinese speak to each other, they will often use this term, which is roughly equivalent to our usage of *Mr., Mrs., Miss* or *Ms.* Chinese do not address foreigners with this term. **Tóng-zhi** is widely used in the People's Republic but *not* in other Chinese-speaking areas, such as Taiwan or Hong Kong or overseas Chinese communities.

2 Getting along in your hotel

The hotel is an excellent place to start applying the Chinese you have learned. The hotel staff will welcome your 'trying out' some Chinese on them just as they will sometimes be anxious to speak a little English to you!

Conversations

Key words and phrases

Do you have any empty rooms?	**Yǒu kòng fáng-jiān ma?**
A double room	**Shuāng-rén-fáng**
Three days	**Sān-tiān**
My passport	**Wǒ-de hù-zhào**

Booking a room

Tourist	Nǐ hǎo.
Receptionist	Nín hǎo.
Tourist	Yǒu kòng fáng-jiān ma?
Receptionist	Yǒu. Nín yào shémma yàngr-de fáng-jiān?
Tourist	Shuāng-rén-fáng.
Receptionist	Nín dǎ-suàn zhù jǐ-tiān?
Tourist	Sān-tiān.
Receptionist	Hǎo. Qǐng ràng wǒ kàn-kàn nǐ-de hù-zhào.
Tourist	Zhè shì wǒ-de hù-zhào.
Receptionist	Xiè-xie.

Key words and phrases

I'm sorry Unfortunately Excuse me	**Duì-bu-qǐ.**
They're all gone.	**Méi-yǒu-le.**

Finding the hotel full

| Tourist | Yǒu kòng fáng-jiān ma? |
| Receptionist | Duì-bu-qǐ. Méi-yǒu-le. |

Key words and phrases

Reserved a room	**Yù-dìng-le fáng-jiān**
On the second floor	**Zài dì-èr-lóu**
Room number	**Fáng-hào**

A room booked in advance

Tourist	Nǐ hǎo.
Receptionist	Nín hǎo.
Tourist	Wǒ yǐ-jīng yù-dìng-le fáng-jiān.
Receptionist	Nín guì-xìng.
Tourist	Wǒ xìng Smith.
Receptionist	Nín hǎo. Huān-yíng, huān-yíng. Nǐ-de fáng-jiān zài dì-èr-lóu.
Tourist	Fáng-hào duō-shǎo?
Receptionist	Èr-sān-sì.
Tourist	Duì-bu-qǐ, qǐng nǐ zài shuō.
Receptionist	Èr-sān-sì.
Tourist	Xiè-xie.

Numbers

one	two	three	four	five
yī	**èr**	**sān**	**sì**	**wǔ**

If you don't understand what people say, ask them to repeat

Qǐng nín zài shuō.   *Please say it again.*

And listen for

Being asked your name

Nín guì-xìng?   *What's your (sur)name?*

And replying

Wǒ xìng Smith.   *My last name is Smith.*

Being asked for how many nights

Nín dǎ-suàn zhù jǐ-tiān?	*How many days are you staying?*
Sān-tiān.	*Three 'nights' (days).*

Being told which floor

Dì-yī-lóu	*First floor*
Dì-èr-lóu	*Second floor*
Dì-sān-lóu.	*Third floor*
Dì-sì-lóu	*Fourth floor*
Dì-wǔ-lóu	*Fifth floor*

And remember these forms (from Program One)

Nín shì nǎ-guó rén?	*What nationality are you?*
Wǒ shi . . . Zhōng-guo rén.	*I'm Chinese.*
Dé-guo rén.	*German.*
Měi-guo rén.	*American.*
Fà-guo rén.	*French.*

Key words and phrases

Traveler's check	**Lǚ-xíng-zhī-piào**
'People's' currency	**Rén-mín-bì**
Fifty dollars	**Wǔ-shí-kuài**
Thanks	**Xiè-xie**
You're welcome	**Bú-xiè**

Changing traveler's checks

Tourist	Nǐ hǎo. Wǒ xiǎng huàn lǚ-xíng-zhī-piào.
Clerk	Hǎo. Duō-shao kuài rén-mín-bì?
Tourist	Wǔ-shí-kuài.
Clerk	Hǎo. Qǐng nín qiān-míng.
Tourist	Hǎo.
Clerk	Qǐng ràng wǒ kàn-kàn nǐ-de hù-zhào.

Tourist	Zhè shì wǒ-de hù-zhào.
Clerk	Zhè shì wǔ-shí-kuài rén-mín-bì.
Tourist	Xiè-xie, xiè-xie, zài-jiàn.
Clerk	Bú-xiè, bú-xiè. Zài-jiàn, zài-jiàn.

Saying ok   fine   all right
Hǎo.

Some more numbers

six	seven	eight	nine	ten
liù	qī	bā	jiǔ	shí

And some higher numbers

twenty	thirty	forty	fifty
èr-shí	sān-shí	sì-shí	wǔ-shí

sixty	seventy	eighty	ninety
liù-shí	qī-shí	bā-shí	jiǔ-shí

And don't forget this form
Nǐ hǎo!   *Hello!*

Saying 'thanks'
Xiè-xie

You're welcome
Bú-xiè

Explanations

How many?

Jǐ-tiān is 'how many days?' Jǐ- is usually used for questions about amounts involving smaller numbers (under ten). Duō-shao also means 'how many' and is used when larger numbers are involved, such as

Duō-shao kuài rén-mín-bì?   *How much in ren-min-bi?*
Wǔ-shí-kuài.   *Fifty dollars.*

'Yes' and 'no' in Chinese

Although Chinese does have words that can be regarded as meaning 'yes' and 'no' (**shì**, yes and **bù-shì**, no), it does not use them to the same extent as English. To answer 'yes,' simply use the basic form of the verb. To indicate 'no,' put **bù·** (meaning 'not') in front of the verb. This applies to all verbs except one: **yǒu** (meaning 'to have'). Its negative form is **méi·yǒu** ('not to have, to be without').

Examples:

Nǐ yào shū ma?	*Do you want some books?*
Yào.	*Yes (I do want some).*
Nǐ yǒu xíng·li ma?	*Do you have any luggage?*
Méi·yǒu.	*No (I do not).*

Locating things in Chinese

Location is expressed in Chinese most often by using the verb **zài** (meaning 'in, at, on'). For example:

Nǐ·de fáng·jiān zài dì·yī·lóu. *Your room is on the first floor.*

Hotel rooms

A single room is **dān·rén·fáng**; a double, **shuāng·rén·fáng**; and a room with two beds is **liǎng·zhāng chúang·de fáng·jiān**. If you want a room with a shower, you should ask for — **yǒu lín·yù·de fáng·jiān**.

Exercises

1   The following conversation is one you might have if you were trying to book a room in a hotel. The receptionist's part is written out for you. Work out your part of the conversation.

You	(Hello) _____
Receptionist	Nǐ hǎo.
You	(Do you have any empty rooms?) _____ _____
Receptionist	Yǒu. Nín yào shémma yàngr·de fáng·jiān.
You	(A single) _____
Receptionist	Nín dǎ·suàn zhù jǐ·tiān?
You	(Four days) _____

Receptionist	Hǎo.
You	(How much in ren-min-bi?) _____
	_____
Receptionist	Bā-shí-kuài.
You	(OK) _____
Receptionist	Qǐng ràng wǒ kàn-kàn nǐ-de hù-zhào.
You	(This is my passport.) _____
	_____
Receptionist	Xiè-xie.

2 Read the following phrases aloud several times.
   Which phrase goes best with each situation?
   Write the correct number beside each letter.

   a. Qǐng nín shuō   1. What's your
      Zhōng-guo huà.   (sur)name?
   b. Nín guì-xìng?   2. Please help me.
   c. Qǐng bāng-zhù wǒ.   3. I'm American.
   d. Wǒ yào huàn lǚ-xíng-   4. Please speak Chinese.
      zhī-piào.
   e. Wǒ shì Měi-guo rén.   5. I want to cash
                                traveler's checks.

3. Convert these numbers into Chinese:

   five ten three two twenty forty one six
   seven nine fifty four eight thirty

4. You've just come back to the hotel and want to
   ask for your key. Practice these room numbers
   aloud, and then convert them to English.

   bā-sān-sì
   yī-èr-wǔ
   wǔ-qī-bā
   sān-sì-liù
   bā-qī-jiǔ
   liù-sān-sì

5 You're talking with someone you have met in
   China. Answer his questions.

   Friend Nín hǎo.
   You   (Hello)

Friend	Nín shì nǎ-guó rén?
You	(I'm American)
Friend	Nín guì-xìng?
You	(I'm surnamed Johnson) (Yūe-hàn-shēn)
Friend	Yūe-hàn-shēn xiān-sheng, nín hǎo. Wǒ xìng Zhāng.
You	(How do you do, Mr. Zhang)

Worth knowing

Hotels

For detailed information on hotels and for many other aspects of a visit to China, you should consult a travel agent and also purchase a good guidebook. Take the guidebook to China with you. One good one is Fodor's *People's Republic of China* (McKay Publishing, 1983). At the height of the travel season (spring and early summer), you'd be advised to book through an agent or travel with a tour. The Chinese International Travel Service (Zhōng-guó Gúo-jì Lǚ-xíng-shè) now arranges most hotel bookings well in advance for travelers to China. You will generally have little choice of accommodations, but standards are improving. Here are some features of tourist-oriented hotels in China.

Laundry

Same-day laundry services are usually available and adequate for general travel purposes. Dry cleaning is also available, but the quality may not be high.

Hairdressers

The larger tourist hotels will have good hairdressing salons for both men and women (separate facilities) at very reasonable rates. Do not, however, expect elaborate styling.

Service desks

A service desk (**fú·wù·tái**) is common on each floor of the larger hotels, where the traveler can pick up laundry, drinks, ice, and book phone calls and get a variety of other services.

Chinesě money

Chinese currency is called **rén·mín·bì**, 'People's (**rén·mín**) Currency (**bì**).' Paper currency is denominated into notes of one, two, five and ten. The basic unit or 'dollar' is sometimes referred to in Chinese as **yúan** but more often is called **kuài** in the spoken language. So **duō·shao kuài rén·mín·bì?** or 'how much in People's currency?'

3 Getting your shopping done

(Note: Prices of items in this program are not current. Prices change in China just as they do in America. Currency values also shift, so be prepared for this when you get to China.)

Conversations

Key words and phrases

What would you like to buy?	Nǐ mǎi shémma?
I'll buy some . . .	Wǒ mǎi . . .
Chinese wine	Zhōng-guo jiǔ
Two bottles	Liǎng-píng

Buying a bottle of Chinese wine

Shopkeeper	Nǐ hao.
Customer	Nǐ hǎo.
Shopkeeper	Nǐ mǎi shémma?
Customer	Wǒ mǎi zhèi-ge Zhōng-guo jiǔ.
Shopkeeper	Jǐ-píng?
Customer	Liǎng-píng.

The basic numbers again

One	Two	Three	Four	Five
Yī	**Èr**	**Sān**	**Sì**	**Wǔ**
	Liǎng			

Six	Seven	Eight	Nine	Ten
Liù	**Qī**	**Bā**	**Jiǔ**	**Shí**

Four kinds of wine — to practice the four tones

First tone	*Second tone*	*Third tone*	*Fourth tone*
Zhōng-guo jiǔ	**Dé-guo jiǔ**	**Měi-guo jiǔ**	**Fà-guo jiǔ**
Chinese wine	German wine	American wine	French wine

Asking, 'How many?'

Nǐ yào jǐ-ge?	*How many do you want (of anything, under ten in number)?*
Nǐ yào duō-shǎo?	*How many do you want (of anything, usually involving higher numbers)?*
Nǐ yào jǐ-píng?	*How many bottles do you want?*
Liǎng-píng.	*Two bottles.*

If you don't know what something is called

The easiest thing to do is simply point at what you want and say

Zhèi-ge	*This one*

or

Wǒ mǎi zhèi-ge.	*I'll buy/take this one.*

Remember these forms

Zǎo.	*Good morning.*
Zài-jiàn.	*Good-bye.*
Nín hǎo.	*Hello.*

What shopkeepers will ask you

Nín mǎi shémma?	*What will you have?*

And you say . . .

Wǒ mǎi . . .	*I'll have some . . .*

Key words and phrases

A sweater	**Yí-jiàn máo-yī**
Attractive	**Hǎo-kàn**
Don't like it	**Bù-xǐ-huān**
Do you have any others?	**Yǒu bíe-de ma?**

Buying a sweater

Shopkeeper	Nín hǎo.
Customer	Nín hǎo.
Shopkeeper	Nín xiǎng mǎi shémma?
Customer	Wǒ mǎi yí-jiàn máo-yī.
Shopkeeper	Hǎo. Zhèi-jiàn hěn hǎo-kàn. Nǐ xǐ-huān ma?
Customer	Bù-xǐ-huān. Yǒu bíe-de ma?
Shopkeeper	Yǒu. Zhèi-jiàn hǎo-kàn ma?
Customer	Hěn hǎo-kàn. Wǒ mǎi zhèi-jiàn.

Some positives	Some negatives (just use prefix bù-)
mǎi (to buy)	**bù-mǎi**
xǐ-huān (to like)	**bù-xǐ-huān**
hǎo (be good)	**bù-hǎo**
hǎo-kàn (be pretty)	**bù-hǎo-kàn**

When you're asked if you like something

Nǐ xǐ-huān ma?	*Do you like it?*
Wǒ hén xǐ-huān.	*I like it very much.*
Wǒ bù-xǐ-huān.	*I don't like it.*

If you want to see something else, just say

Yǒu bíe-de ma?	*Do you have anything else?*

Even more numbers: (see page 35 for one thru ten)

11	12	13
shí-yī	**shí-èr**	**shí-sān**

14	15	16
shí-sì	**shí-wǔ**	**shí-liù**

17	18	19
shí-qī	shí-bā	shí-jiú

and some more

20	30	40	50
èr-shí	sān-shí	sì-shí	wǔ-shí

60	70	80	90
liù-shí	qī-shí	bā-shí	jiǔ-shí

and even more

21	32	43	54
èr-shí-yī	sān-shí-èr	sì-shí-sān	wǔ-shí-sì

65	76	87	98
liù-shí-wǔ	qī-shí-liù	bā-shí-qī	jiǔ-shí-bā

Key words and phrases

Map	**Dì-tú**
Peking	**Běi-jīng**
Please have a look.	**Qǐng nín kàn-kàn.**
50 cents	**Wǔ-máo qián**

Buying a map

Customer	Yǒu meí-yǒu dì-tú?
Salesgirl	Shémma dì-tú?
Customer	Běi-jīng dì-tú.
Salesgirl	Yǒu. Qǐng nín kàn-kàn.
Customer	Zhèi-ge hén hǎo. Duō shao qián?
Salesgirl	Yí-kuài wǔ-máo jiǔ-fēn qián.
Customer	Xiè-xie, wǒ mǎi yī-ge.

If not sure they have what you want, say . . .

Yǒu méi-yǒu . . .?   *Do you have any . . .?*

And remember this form: asking the price

Duō-shao qián?   *How much?*

Dollars and dimes

one dollar	two dollars	five dollars
yí·kuài qián	**liǎng·kuài qián**	**wǔ·kuài qián**

ten cents	twenty cents	thirty cents
yì·máo qián	**liǎng·máo qián**	**sān·máo qián**

forty cents	fifty cents
sì·máo qián	**wǔ·máo qián**

What to say if you don't understand

Duì-bu-qǐ, qǐng nín zài shuō.

Excuse me, please say it again.

What you need to listen for

Being asked what you want

Nín mǎi shémma?   *What will you have?*

Ní xǐ–huān ma?

Hén xǐ–huān.
Dūo–shao qián?

Being told the price

Sān-kuài, liù-máo, wǔ-fēn qián.   *Three sixty-five.*

Being asked to take a look at something

Qǐng nín kàn-kàn.   *Please have a look (at this).*

What you need to say

Wǒ xiǎng mǎi . . .	*I'd like to buy a . . .*
Duō-shao qián?	*How much?*
Yǒu meí-yǒu . . .?	*Do you have any . . .?*
Wǒ bù-xǐ-huān.	*I don't care for it.*
Yǒu bíe-de ma?	*Do you have any others?*
Wǒ mǎi.	*I'll take it.*

Explanations

To form the negative of any verb in Chinese, just put **bù-** in front of the verb. Here are some examples.

Positive	*Negative*
hǎo	bù-hǎo
hǎo-kàn	bù-hǎo-kàn
mǎi	bù-mǎi
yào	bú-yào
xǐ-huān	bù-xǐ-huān

There's only one exception: the verb **wǒ yǒu** 'to have,' as in **wǒ yǒu qián** 'I have money.' The negative of this verb is formed with the prefix **méi-**. Here are some examples.

Positive	*Negative*
yǒu	méi-yǒu
yǒu qián	méi-yǒu qián
yǒu bíe-de ma?	méi-yǒu bíe-de?
yǒu sān-ge	méi-yǒu sān-ge
yǒu dì-tú ma?	méi-yǒu dì-tú

Exercises

1 The clerk says **Nǐ hǎo** to you and asks what you want. You wish to buy some Chinese wine. Choose the correct one.

    a. Dé-guo jiǔ.
    b. Zhōng-guo jiǔ.
    c. Fà-guo jiǔ.
    d. Měi-guo jiǔ.

2 You go into a small shop, and the shopkeeper says, **Xiān-sheng zǎo. Nín xiǎng mǎi shémma?** Does he mean

    a. Good evening. What do you want?
    b. Good morning. What do you want to buy?
    c. Good morning. How are you?

3 You want to ask for a map of China. Do you say,

    a. Běi-jīng dì-tú.
    b. Yì-píng Zhōng-guó jiǔ.
    c. Zhōng-guo dì-tú.

4 The shopkeeper gives you the map and says, **Jiǔ-máo qián**. Is he saying,

    a. We're all out.
    b. Ninety cents.
    c. Please have a look at it.

5 You want to know if the shop has any sweaters. Do you say,

    a. Duō-shao qián?
    b. Yǒu méi-yǒu máo-yī?
    c. Yǒu béi-de ma?

6 You do find a sweater you like and want to know how much it costs. Do you say,

    a. Nín hǎo ma?
    b. Nǐ yǒu bíe-de ma?
    c. Duō-shao qián?

7 He says that the sweater costs **sān-kuài qián**. Is that

    a. Four dollars.
    b. Sixty cents.
    c. Three dollars.

8 You're doing some shopping. Ask for the following items:

    a. three sweaters.
    b. six maps.
    c. two bottles of Chinese wine.

9 Here are the prices for the preceding items. Provide the Chinese for each, and work out the total.

    a. three sweaters — nine dollars.
    b. two maps — one dollar.
    c. two bottles of Chinese wine — five dollars.

10 You're buying some gifts for the family at the Friendship Store (**Yóu-yì-Shāng-diàn**) and trying out some Chinese at the same time. Complete this dialogue by filling in what you would say to the clerk.

First greet the clerk.

You	(Hello.) _____
Clerk	Nín hǎo. Nín xiǎng mǎi shémma?
You	(Ask her if she has any sweaters.) ____ _____
Clerk	Yǒu. Nǐ xǐ-huān zhèi-jiàn ma?
You	(Say you don't care for it. Ask her if she has any others.) _____ _____
Clerk	Yǒu. Zhèi-jiàn hèn hǎo-kàn. Nín xǐ-huān ma?
You	(Say you like it very much, and ask the price.)_____
Clerk	Shí-bā-kuài qián.
You	(Say you'll take it, thank her and say good-bye.)_____

11 First practice saying the following questions aloud, and then supply the answers suggested in parentheses.

   a. Nín xiǎng mǎi shémma? (I'd like to buy a sweater.)
   b. Zhèi-ge duō-shao qián? (Twenty dollars.)
   c. Nín yào jǐ-ge? (I want three.)
   d. Nǐ yǒu bié-de ma? (Yes, we have.)
   e. Zhèi-ge hǎo-kàn ma? (It's very good-looking.)
   f. Nín xiǎng mǎi ma? (I would like to buy it very much.)
   g. Nín yào jǐ-píng? (I want six bottles.)
   h. Nín xǐ-huān zhèi-ge ma? (I like it a lot.)
   i. Yǒu méi-yǒu dì-tú? (We have no maps.)

12 You're shopping. The shop assistant says, **Nín xiǎng mǎi shémma?** Are you being

   a. asked if you want anything else?
   b. asked what you wish to buy?
   c. asked which size you want?

   Nǐ yào jǐ-píng? Are you being

   a. offered a bag for wrapping?
   b. asked how many bottles you want?
   c. asked what you wish to buy?

   Bā-kuài qián Are you being

   a. asked if you want anything else?
   b. told that the bill comes to eight dollars?
   c. told they have no maps?

Worth knowing

Names of shops

gǔ-wán-diàn	*antique shop*
bǎi-huò-shāng-diàn	*department store*
shū-diàn	*bookstore*
fú-zhuāng-diàn	*clothing store*
gōng-yì měi-shù shāng-diàn	*handicrafts shop*

And some gifts

zhū-bǎo-hé	*jewel box*
jǐng-tài-lán	*cloisonné*
máo-bǐ	*Chinese brush pen*
tuō-xíe	*slippers*
hàn-sǎn	*parasol*

More on Chinese money

In Program Two we told you a few facts about Chinese currency (**rén-mín-bì**), which is denominated into **kuài** (dollars), **máo** (dimes) and **fēn** (cents). Starting in 1979, the Chinese government began to issue 'certificates' to foreign tourists in exchange for foreign currency. These are very roughly equivalent to the Chinese version of 'traveler's checks.' A tourist will turn in the 'certificates' when he or she leaves China, getting his own national currency in exchange.

4 Getting something to eat

Conversations

Key words and phrases

Welcome!	**Huān-yíng!**
Table	**zhuō-zi**
Fine, fine!	**Kéyi, kéyi!**

Getting a table

Tourist   Ní hǎo.
Waiter   Ní hǎo. Huān-yíng, huān-yíng. Jǐ-wèi a?
Tourist   Yí-gòng bā-ge rén.
Waiter   Zhèi-ge zhuō-zi kéyi ma?
Tourist   Kéyi.

If someone asks you, 'Is this OK?'

Kéyi ma?	*Is this OK? Is this all right with you?*
Kéyi.	*Fine.*

If it's not OK,

Bù-kéyi.

Key words and phrases

Menu	**Cài-dān**
English menu	**Yīng-wén-de cài-dān**
Here it is.	**Zhè jiù-shì.**

Getting a menu

Customer	Ní hǎo.
Waiter	Ní hǎo.
Customer	Qǐng gěi wǒ Yīng-wén-de cài-dān.
Waiter	Hǎo. Zhè jiù-shì.
Customer	Xiè-xie.

And don't forget these phrases

Qǐng gěi wǒ . . .	*Please give me . . .*
Qǐng bāng-zhù wǒ . . .	*Please help me . . .*

Key words and phrases

Order food	**Diǎn cài**
Four main dishes and one soup	**Sì-ge cài, yí-ge tāng**
Chicken, duck, fish, bean curd	**Jī, yā, yú, dòu-fu**
Rice	**Mǐ-fàn**

Ordering dinner

Tourist	Wáng xīan-sheng, qǐng nǐ bāng-zhù wǒmen diǎn cài.
Wáng xīan-sheng	Kéyì. Wǒmen shì wǔ-ge rén. Sì-ge cài, yí-ge tāng, hǎo bù-hǎo?
Tourist	Hěn hǎo.
Wáng xīan-sheng	Fú-wù-yuán tóng-zhì, wǒmen yào diǎn cài.
Fú-wù-yuán	Nǐmen xiǎng chī shémma?
Wáng xīan-sheng	Wǒmen yào yí-ge* gōng-bǎo jī-dīng, yí-ge Běi-jīng kǎo-yā, yí-ge hóng-shāo yú, yí-ge bái-cài dòu-fu. Hái yào yí-ge sān-xiān tāng. Dōu chī mǐ-fàn.

---

*Mr. Wang here orders 'one of' (**yí-ge**) each main dish. The main courses are each served in individual large dishes, from which all the diners help themselves with their own chopsticks.

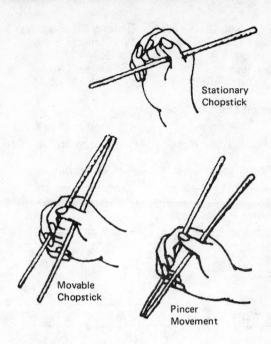

Stationary Chopstick

Movable Chopstick

Pincer Movement

Some food you might enjoy

gōng-bǎo jī-dīng *hot and spicy chicken*
Běi-jīng kǎo-yā *Peking duck*
hóng-shāo yú *red-cooked fish*
bái-cài dòu-fu *bean curd with (Chinese) cabbage*

Expressing your likes

Wǒ xiǎng chī . . . *I'd like to have some . . . to eat.*

Wǒ xiǎng chī jī. *I'd like to have some chicken.*

and dislikes

Wǒ bù-xiǎng chī jī. *I'd rather not have chicken. I don't want chicken.*

What do you like to eat? **Nǐ xiǎng chī shémma?**
I'd like to have some   *Wǒ xiǎng chī Běi-jīng*
Peking duck.   *kǎo-yā.*
I'd like fish.   *Wǒ xiǎng chī yú.*
I'd like bean curd.   *Wǒ xiǎng chī dòu-fu.*

Different kinds of food

jī	kǎo-yā	yú	dòu-fu	mǐ-fàn
chicken	*roast duck*	*fish*	*bean curd*	*rice*

And don't forget how to address restaurant help

Fú-wù-yuán tóng-zhì   *'comrade assistant'*

Ordering a glass of water

Qǐng gěi wǒ yì-bēi shuǐ.   *Please give me a glass of*
                             water.

Key words

To drink	**Hē**
Beer	**Pí-jiǔ**
Two bottles	**Liǎng-píng**
Tea	**Chá**
Coffee	**Kā-fēi**

Getting something to drink

Beer

Waiter   Nǐmen xiǎng hē shémma?
Tourist Wǒmen xiǎng hē pí-jiǔ.
Waiter   Hǎo. Jǐ-píng?
Tourist Liǎng-píng.

Tea and coffee

Fú-wù-yuán   Nǐmen xiǎng hē shémma?
Young man   Wǒ hē chá.
Fú-wù-yuán   Xiǎo-jie, nǐ hē chá ma?
Young lady   Bù-hē chá. Wǒ hē kā-fēi.

A cup of this and a glass of that . . .

Yì-bēi chá	*a cup of tea*
Yì-bēi kā-fēi	*a cup of coffee*
Yì-bēi shuǐ	*a glass of water*
Yì-píng pí-jiǔ	*a bottle of beer*

Key words and phrases

Chopsticks	**Kuài-zi**
To use chopsticks	**Yòng kuài-zi**

Using chopsticks

Mr. Wáng	Nǐmen xiǎng yòng kuài-zi ma?
Tourist	Hǎo. Qíng nǐ, jiāo wǒmen, zěmma yòng, hǎo-bu-hǎo?
Wáng	Hǎo.

Key words and phrases

Make out the bill	**Kāi zhàng-dān**
This is it.	**Zhè jiù-shì.**

Paying the bill

Woman	Qíng nǐ kāi zhàng-dān.
Fú-wù-yuán	Zhè jiù-shì. Yí-gòng èr-shí-kuài qián.
Woman	Hǎo. Zhè shì èr-shí-kuài qián.
Fú-wù-yuán	Xiè-xie, xiè-xie. Zài-jiàn.

Exercises

1 Read these orders for food and drink out loud, and then match them with the orders in English from the following list.

   1. yì-píng pí-jiǔ
   2. sān-bēi chá
   3. yì-bēi kā-fēi

   a. a bottle of beer
   b. a cup of coffee
   c. three cups of tea

2 You're eating out with a friend. Work out your part of the conversation:

You	(call for the menu) _____
Waiter	Zhè jiù-shì cài-dān. Nǐmen xiǎng chī shémma?
You	(One order of hot-spicy chicken and one order of cabbage with bean curd)
	_____
Waiter	Nǐmen xiǎng hē shémma?
You	(Two bottles of Qīng-dǎo beer.) _____
	_____
Waiter	Hǎo.
You	(We also want two glasses of water.)
	_____
You	(Call for the bill.) _____
Waiter	Zhè jiù-shì zhàng-dān. Yí-gòng sān-kuài qián.
You	(Here's three dollars.) _____
You	(Thank you. Good-bye.) _____
Waiter	Zài-jiàn.

3 You're in a restaurant with a group of friends, all of whom want different dishes. Have each of the friends tell the waiter what he or she would like to eat.

a. I'd like to have red-cooked fish.
b. I want Peking duck.
c. I'd like some cabbage with bean curd.
d. I want one order of gōng-bǎo chicken.

4 You're in a restaurant, and you need the kind of help described as follows. Supply the phrases.

a. Please help us order food.
b. Please give us an English menu.
c. Please make out the bill.
d. Please teach me how to use chopsticks.

5 Complete these phrases with a suitable word from the list.

1. liǎng-píng (beer)
2. xiǎng chī (Peking duck)

3. bāng-zhù wǒ (order food)
4. wo xiǎng hē (tea)
5. wo xiǎng yòng (chopsticks)

a. diǎn cài
b. chá
c. Běi-jīng kǎo-yā
d. pí-jiǔ
e. kuài-zi

6 Supply the appropriate Chinese for the following situations.

   a. You've just come down to breakfast. Greet the person at the next table.
   b. You've had a busy day. Order a cup of coffee.
   c. You've just finished some light refreshments with Mr. Wang. Say good-bye to him.
   d. You enter a restaurant, and the waiter says, **Jǐ-wèi a?** Say there are five people in your party.

7 You go to a restaurant. You're offered beer but would rather drink tea. What do you say?

   a. liǎng-bēi pí-jiǔ.
   b. wǒ bù-hē pí-jiǔ. wǒ hē chá.
   c. xiè-xie. zài-jiàn.

8 The waiter asks what you will have. You tell him you want to see the menu. What do you say?

   a. xiǎng hē jiǔ.
   b. xiǎng kàn cài-dān.
   c. xiǎng chī jī.

9 You call the waiter over and ask him to make out the bill. What do you say?

   a. duō-shao qián?
   b. wǒ xiǎng chī dòu-fu.
   c. qǐng nǐ kāi zhàng-dān.

10 You are the only one who knows any Chinese. Order drinks for everyone. Figure out what each order is, then total them up and tell the waiter.

Don't forget to order something for yourself.

a. a bottle of beer and a cup of coffee
b. one bottle of beer, a cup of coffee and a cup of tea
c. a cup of coffee

Worth knowing

Food

The major varieties of Chinese food include the following:

☐ northern style (**Běi-fāng cài**) or Peking style (**Běi-jīng cài**). This style tends to be somewhat oilier; and the dishes, spicier and saltier. There are more meat dishes, such as lamb and lots of dumplings, noodles and buns.

☐ southern style (**nán-fāng cài**) or Canton style (**Guǎng-dōng cài**). Food served in this style tends to have greater visual appeal than the northern variety. Specialties include fish and seafoods, but meat dishes are equally delightful.

☐ Szechuan style (**Sì-chuān cài**). **Sì-chuān** is a southwestern province of China noted for its spicy-hot food. Many dishes are very hot, so you'll want to take it easy.

Drinks

Most brands of local beer are quite good. The most popular 'brews' are the 'Tsing Tao' (**Qīng-Dǎo**) and 'Peking' brands. Western liquors are not widely available, so some travelers prefer to bring their own.

At banquets you will be served **Máo tái** (rice) wine for toasting only. It's quite strong, so be careful. The **Shào Xīng** red rice wine is less potent.

Naturally, there are many varieties of tea available. Sample as many as you can and bring a tin home with you.

Coffee in China is often a disappointment. So bring your own jar of instant.

5 Getting around

Conversations

Key words and phrases

Museum	**bó-wù-guǎn**
Where?	**Zài nǎ-li?**
Go right.	**Wàng yòu-biān zǒu.**
Three blocks	**sān-tíao jīe**

Asking where the museum is

Tourist	Qǐng wèn, bó-wù-guǎn zài nǎ-li?
Girl	Nín wàng yòu-biān zǒu, guò-sān-tíao jīe, jiù dào-le.
Tourist	Xiè-xie, xiè-xie.
Girl	Bú-xiè.

Always precede your questions with

Qǐng wèn . . .?	*May I ask . . .?*

Getting someone's attention

Duì-bu-qǐ . . .	*Excuse me . . .*

Or

Qǐng wèn . . .	*May I ask . . .?*

On the left
zuǒ-biān

On the right
yòu-biān

And remember these forms

Thank you!	*You're welcome!*
Xiè-xie! or Xiè-xie nǐ!	Bú-xiè.

Key words and phrases

How do I get to . . .?	**. . . zémma zǒu?**
At the intersection . . .	**Dào-le lù-kǒu . . .**
Speak more slowly.	**Màn yi-dian shuō.**

Finding Tian-an-men Square

First Man	Qǐng wèn, Tīan-ān-mén Guǎng-chǎng, zémma zǒu.
Second Man	Dào-le lù-kǒu, wàng zuǒ-biān zǒu, guò liǎng-tíao jīe, jiù dào-le.
First Man	Qǐng nín màn yi-diǎn shuō.
Second Man	Dào-le lù-kǒu, wàng zǔo-biān zǒu, guò liǎng-tíao, jīe, jiù dào-le.

If they're speaking too fast, you can say

Qǐng nín màn yi-diǎn shuō.

Key words and phrases

Nearby	**Fù-jìn**
Is there a . . .?	**Yǒu méi-yǒu . . .?**
Go straight ahead.	**Wàng qián zǒu.**

Is there a restaurant nearby?

Tourist	Qǐng wèn, fù-jìn yǒu méi-yǒu fàn-guǎr?
Man	Yǒu. Wàng qián zǒu. Dào-le dì-èr-ge lù-kǒu, wàng yòu-biān zǒu, jiù kàn-jian-le.

The first . . .	The second . . .	The third . . .
dì-yī-ge	dì-èr-ge	dì-sān-ge

Keep these phrases in mind

. . . zài nǎ-li?	*Where is the . . . ?*
. . . zémma zǒu?	*How do I get to . . . ?*
Fù-jìn yǒu méi-yǒu . . . ?	*Is there a . . . nearby?*

Key words and phrases

Go to see	**Qù kàn**
Today	**Jīn-tiān**
May I . . . ?	**Kéyi . . . ma?**

Finding out about the tour

Tourist	Wǒmen jīn-tiān qù kàn shémma dì-fāng?
Guide	Wǒmen jīn-tiān qù kàn Wàn-lǐ Cháng-chéng.
Tourist	Kéyi zhào-xiàng ma?
Guide	Kéyi.

To ask permission to do something

Kéyi . . . ma?	*May (I/we) . . . ?*
Kéyi zhào-xiàng ma?	*May (I/we) take photos?*

| Kéyi qù ma? | *May (I/we) go?* |
| Kéyi kàn·kàn ma? | *May (I/we) take a look?* |

And finally,

Yí·lù·píng·ān

'On the whole journey may you have peace'

Have a good trip!

Explanations

Asking the way

When you stop someone to ask him or her the way, you can say, **Duì·bu·qǐ** or **Qǐng wèn**, 'excuse me' or 'May I ask . . .?' To ask the way to somewhere specific, you first say the place you want to get to, followed by **. . . zémma zǒu**, 'How do I get to . . .?' To ask more generally if there's, say, a hotel nearby, it's **fù·jìn yǒu méi·yǒu . . .?** 'Is there a . . . nearby?'

Here are some places you might want to find

yín·háng	*bank*
gōng·yuán	*park*
shì zhōng·xīn	*city center*
yóu·jú	*post office*
chē·zhàn	*train* or *bus station*
bǎi·huò dà·lóu	*department store*
diàn·yǐng·yuàn	*movie theater*

Understanding the reply

You probably won't understand every word of the reply, so listen for the key words and phrases.

wàng qián zǒu	*go straight ahead*
wàng yòu·biān zǒu	*go right*
wàng zuǒ·biān zǒu	*go left*
dào·le lù·kǒu	*at the intersection*

and

| dì·yī·ge, dì·èr·ge, dì·sān·ge | *first, second and third* |

Exercises

1 Ask if there is one of the following places nearby:

a. post office (yóu-jú)
b. bank (yín-háng)
c. park (gōng-yuán)
d. restaurant (fàn-guǎr)
e. department store (bǎi-huò dà-lóu)

2 You want to visit the museum and need to find out where it is. Fill in the gaps in the conversation.

You	(May I ask how to get to the museum?) _____
Passerby	Wàng yòu-biān zǒu, guò yī-tíao jīe, jiù dào-le.
You	(Please speak a little more slowly.)
	_____
Passerby	Wàng yòu-biān zǒu, guò yī-tíao jīe, jiù dào-le.
You	(Thank you. Good-bye.) _____
	_____
Passerby	Bú-xiè.

3 You remember that you must buy some gifts at the Friendship Store (**Yǒu-yì Shāng-diàn**). Ask your Chinese friend if there is one nearby.

You	(Is there a Friendship Store nearby?) _____
Friend	Yǒu. Qǐng nín wàng zuǒ-biān zǒu, guò sì-tíao jīe, yǐ-hòu, (afterward) wàng yòu-biān zǒu, jiù kàn-jian-le.

Based on what your friend said, answer the following questions:

a. Is there a Friendship Store nearby?
b. Must you first go left and then right or right and then left?
c. How many streets must you pass by?

4 What are you being advised to do?

1. wàng qián zǒu
   a. Go left.
   b. Go right.
   c. Go straight ahead.

2. guò sì-tíao jīe
   a. Go four blocks.
   b. Go to the intersection.
   c. Go straight ahead.

3. qǐng màn yi-diǎn shūo
   a. Please go to the left.
   b. Please take this road.
   c. Please speak more slowly.

5 You want to go to Tian-an-men Square. Stop someone and ask politely

   a. _____

   b. The response is: wàng qián zǒu, dào-le lù-kǒu, wàng zuǒ-biān zǒu, guò wǔ-tíao jīe, jiù kàn-jian-le.

   Which way do you turn at the intersection?

6 You are at the spot marked on the map. Using the following directions find out where you end up.

   1. Dào-le dì-èr-ge lù-kǒu, wàng zuǒ-biān zǒu, guò liǎng-tíao jīe, jiù dào-le.

   2. Dào-le dì-sān-ge lù-kǒu, wàng zuǒ-biān zǒu, guò liǎng-tíao jīe, jiù kàn-jiàn-le.

   3. Dào-le dì-èr-ge lù-kǒu, wàng zuǒ-biān zǒu, guò yì-tíao jīe, jiù dào-le.

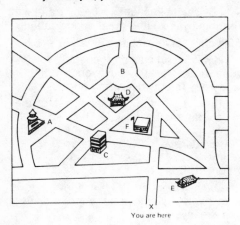

X
You are here

Key to Map

A Bó-wù-guǎn (museum)
B Tīan-ān-mén Guǎng-chǎng (Tian-an-men Square)
C Běi-jīng Fàn-diàn (Peking Hotel)
D Fàn-guǎr (restaurant)
E Yào-diàn (drugstore)
F Yóu-jú (post office)

7 Now work out your own directions to get to

    a. restaurant (fàn-guǎr)
    b. post office (yóu-jú)
    c. drugstore (yào-diàn)

Worth knowing

Travel in China

Train tickets must be booked in advance through **Zhōng-guó Lǚ-xíng-shè** (China International Travel Service). Your hotel receptionist can act as your intermediary. Foreign tourists usually have special cars reserved for them, often with special comfort features.

You'll usually book the **tè-kuài-chē** (express train) with 'soft class' seating (**ruǎn-xí**) (the most comfortable).

Dining cars (**cān-chē**) serve excellent food.

Buses (**chē** or **gōng-gōng-qì-chē**) are generally very crowded. If you plan to travel by bus work out the details of the journey in advance with your guide.

Taxis can be arranged through the lobby desk of the hotel. Drivers do not usually speak English, so tell the dispatcher where you want to go, or get the desk clerk to write down the address in Chinese for you. There are no meters in the cab, but the drivers are scrupulously honest. *Don't tip.*

Bicycling is the best way of seeing the sights, but be careful of the many, many bikes on the street. Getting a bike is also not easy.

Walking is also a good way to sample the nearby sights, especially those in the vicinity of your hotel. Don't wander *too* far.

If you get stuck somewhere, contact your hotel. Carry the hotel number with you at all times.

Can you 'GET BY?'

Test

Try these exercises when you've finished the course. The answers are on page 74.

1 Provide in Chinese a suitable greeting for each of these situations.

   a You meet Mr. Wáng at a dinner party in the evening.

   b You meet your friend Miss Lǐ by chance in a bookshop.

   c You go into a travel agency at 9:00 A.M.

   d You leave a group of friends at a restaurant to go back to your hotel.

   e You meet Mrs. Lǐ in the early morning just after breakfast.

2 a You meet your guide's wife for the first time. How do you say, 'How do you do!'? _____

   b After not seeing your friend Mr. Zhào for two weeks, you run into him while shopping. How do you say, 'Hello, how are you?' _____

   c Now you meet Mr. Zhào's brother, who asks, 'Ní hǎo ma?' How do you say, 'I'm well, thanks. How about you?' _____

3 Read the following questions and requests out loud, and then choose the situation in which you might say them from the following list.

   1. Qíng nǐ shuō Yīng-wén.

   2. Qíng nǐ bāng-zhù wǒ.

   3. Duì-bu-qǐ, duì-bu-qǐ!

   4. Nín guì-xìng?

   5. Nín shì nǎ-guó rén?

   6. Yǒu kòng fáng-jiān ma?

   7. Qǐng ràng wǒ kàn-kàn nǐ-de hù-zhào.

   8. Fáng-hào duō-shǎo?

9. Qǐng nín zài shuō.
10. Qǐng nín qiān-míng.

a When you need someone's help.
b Being asked what your nationality is.
c When you ask what the room number is.
d Getting someone's attention.
e Asking someone to speak English.
f Requesting that something be said once again.
g Being asked to sign your name.
h Asking if the hotel has any empty rooms.
i Being asked to show your passport.
j Asking someone his or her last name.

4 You're in a **fàn-guǎr** (restaurant), and a group of friends want you to show off your Chinese and do all the ordering. How do you ask for

a a menu
b three beers
c two cups of tea
d one cup of coffee
e a glass of water

5 You're out shopping. How do you ask for these items?

a two bottles of Chinese wine
b a map of Peking
c a sweater

6 You've just arrived in town, and you want to find a hotel and some other places nearby. How do you ask

a Where is the museum?
b How do I get to Tian-an-men Square?
c Is there a restaurant nearby?
d Where is the bank (yín-háng)?
e Is there a post office (yóu-jú) nearby?
f Where is the department store (bǎi-huò dà-lóu)?

7 Look at the following sets of directions. Pick out the key words and note down the way you have to go.

a wàng yòu-biān zǒu

b dào-le lù-kǒu, wàng zuǒ-biān zǒu

c guò liǎng-tíao jīe, jiù dào-le

d dào-le dì-yi-ge lù-kǒu, wàng yòu-biān zǒu

e guò sì-tíao jīe, wàng zuǒ-biān zǒu

f dào-le lù-kǒu, wàng yòu-biān zǒu, jiù kàn-jian-le

8 Read the following prices out loud, and then write
   down in figures how much they are.
   a liǎng-kuài qián
   b sān-máo qián
   c wǔ-fēn qián
   d shí-wǔ-kuài qián
   e sì-kuài liǎng-máo wǔ-fēn qián
   f yī-kuài bā-máo wǔ-fēn qián
   g shí-sì-kuài qián

9 What might you say when you're asked
   a Nǐ xiǎng chī shémma?
   b Nǐ xǐ-huan chī jī ma?
   c Nǐ yào hē kā-fēi ma?
   d Nǐ mǎi jǐ-píng Zhōng-guo jiǔ?
   e Nǐ xǐ-huan zhèi-ge máo-yī ma?

10 What would you say if . . .
   a you are asking the price of something.
   b you decide to buy this one.
   c you want to know where the hotel (lǚ-guǎn) is.
   d you want to know how to get to the Peking
      Hotel (Běi-jīng Fàn-diàn).
   e you ask someone to repeat what has just been
      said.
   f you would like to have a cup of coffee.
   g you want to identify yourself as American.
   h you would like someone to speak Chinese.
   i you ask if the shop has maps (for sale).

Reference section

Extra grammar notes

Language

Roughly 75 percent of the population of China speak the most common form of Chinese, often called Mandarin in the West, but called **pǔ-tōng-huà** ('common speech') in China. The Chinese you hear in these programs is typical Mandarin, understandable throughout most of China, especially in the major cities. There are, of course, many local dialects and varieties of pronunciation, but you will certainly be understood when you speak the Chinese you've learned in this course.

Adjectives

Adjectives precede the noun they qualify.

hǎo rén	*good person*
kòng fáng-jiān	*empty room*

Verbs

There are no verb endings to worry about in Chinese. Verbs that have appeared in the conversations have been translated for you as they arise in the context. The words for *I*, *you*, *we*, etc., are often omitted in Chinese.

qù kàn	*go to see*
qù kàn Wàn-lǐ Cháng-chéng	*go to see the Great Wall*

The verb does not change on account of tense. Tense change is indicated by the addition of word-particles such as **le** (**dào-le lù-kǒu . . .**)('(After) you've *reached* the corner . . .'). If you want to look further into this feature of Chinese, we suggest a more advanced course. The notes we provide here are meant only to 'get you by.'

Numbers

0	lǐng	10	shí				
1	yī	11	shí-yī				
2	èr	12	shí-èr	20	èr-shí		
3	sān	13	shí-sān	30	sān-shí		
4	sì	14	shí-sì	40	sì-shí		
5	wǔ	15	shí-wǔ	50	wǔ-shí		
6	liù	16	shí-liù	60	liù-shí		
7	qī	17	shí-qī	70	qī-shí		
8	bā	18	shí-bā	80	bā-shí		
9	jiǔ	19	shí-jiǔ	90	jiǔ-shí		

100	yì-bǎi	600	liù-bǎi	1000	yì-qiān
200	liǎng-bǎi	700	qī-bǎi	2000	liǎng-qiān
300	sān-bǎi	800	bā-bǎi	3000	sān-qiān
400	sì-bǎi	900	jiǔ-bǎi	4000	sì-qiān
500	wǔ-bǎi				

Days of the week

The *first* day of the week in China is Monday.

xīng-qī-yī	*Monday*
xīng-qī-èr	*Tuesday*
xīng-qī-sān	*Wednesday*
xīng-qī-sì	*Thursday*
xīng-qī-wǔ	*Friday*
xīng-qī-liù	*Saturday*
xīng-qī-tiān	*Sunday*

Months of the year

'Month' in Chinese is **yuè**. This word is preceded by the numbers one through twelve to form the months of the year.

yī-yuè	*January*
èr-yuè	*February*
sān-yuè	*March*

sì-yuè	*April*
wǔ-yuè	*May*
liù-yuè	*June*
qī-yuè	*July*
bā-yuè	*August*
jiǔ-yuè	*September*
shí-yuè	*October*
shí-yī-yuè	*November*
shí-èr-yuè	*December*

Seasons of the year

chūn-tiān	*spring*
xià-tiān	*summer*
qiū-tiān	*autumn*
dōng-tiān	*winter*

Years

The easiest way to say the year is to give the numbers of the year 'telephone style,' that is, number by number: one nine eight three — 1983, followed by the word for 'year' in Chinese, **-nián**.

1980	yī jiǔ bā lǐng nián
1981	yī jiǔ bā yī nián
1982	yī jiǔ bā èr nián
1983	yī jiǔ bā sān nián
1984	yī jiǔ bā sì nián

Sign language

Most signs are printed in Chinese characters, but recently there has been an increasing use of PINYIN spelling alongside Chinese characters. Here are some of the most common.

Airport	Fēi-jī-chǎng
Bus Station	Chē-zhàn
Open	Kāi-mén
Closed	Guān-mén
Danger Zone	Wēi-xiǎn-qū
Entrance	Rù-kǒu
Exit	Chū-kǒu
For Hire	Chū-zū
Ladies' Room	Nǚ cè-suǒ
Men's Room	Nán cè-suǒ
No photographs	Jìn-zhǐ shè-yǐng
No admittance	Jìn-zhǐ rù-nèi
No smoking	Jìn-zhǐ xī-yān

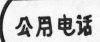

Gōng-yòng Diàn-hùa
(Public Telephone)

公共厕所

Gōng-gòng Cè-sǔo
(Public Rest-room)

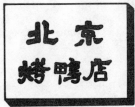

Běi-jīng
Kǎo-yā dìan
(Peking Roast Duck
Restaurant)

The written language of China

Fascinating as the subject may be, it is considerably beyond the scope of this book to provide the reader with more than the barest outline of the Chinese written language. First, here's an example of what modern Chinese looks like in written form.

纪念伟大的革命先行者孙中山先生!

纪念他在中国民主革命准备时期，以鲜明的中国革命民主派立场，同中国改良派作了尖锐的斗争。他在这一场斗争中是中国革命民主派的旗帜。

As you can see, the written language is composed of many, many individual 'characters,' which singly and in combinations of twos and threes form 'words' in Chinese. To be able to read modern Chinese fluently, one must have mastered at least three thousand individual characters and the many more thousands of words formed with the basic three thousand. Learning to read takes years of study.

Many characters developed from simple picturelike figures that conveyed meaning. Following is the evolution of the character for 'fish' (**yú**) from ancient times (around 1500 B.C.) to the present day.

yú

 About 1500 B.C.

 About 200 B.C.

 About A.D. 100

 The present character

As you can see, the process has been one of increased simplification, so much so that what looked very much like a fish centuries ago hardly looks that way now. In what follows, you will find some other characters as they are written today and as they were written centuries ago. Can you make out the picture and derive meaning from it?

Then	Now		
亻	人	person	**rén** (This is a simple stick figure of a man walking.)
㚢	女	woman	**nǚ** (The drawing is of a kneeling woman with her arms crossed modestly.)
孚	子	child	**zǐ** (The picture originally showed a person with a large head, i.e., a child.)
木	木	tree, wood	**mù** (The drawing is a stylized picture of a tree.)
⊙	日	sun, day	**rì** (The original character was a drawing of the sun with a dot in the middle.)
☽	月	moon, month	**yuè** (The drawing was of a crescent moon.)
山	山	mountain	**shān** (The early character clearly shows mountain peaks.)

Two characters can be combined to form additional characters with different meanings. For example:

好	to be good	**hǎo** (combines a woman with her child)
森	forest	**lín** (combines three trees)
明	bright	**míng** (combines the sun and the moon)

Can you guess the meaning of the following characters?

1. 安 **ān** — Hint: the top part is a 'roof' with a woman underneath.

2. 休 **xiū** — Hint: a 'person' standing by a tree.

3. 信 **xin** — Hint: the left side is a 'person,' and the right means 'words.'

Two or more characters can combine to form new concepts. Try to guess the meaning of the following combinations.

4. 山水 **shān-shuǐ** — Hint: the word for mountain (shān) with the word for river (shuǐ).

5. 电话 **diàn-huà** — Hint: the first character means 'electric'; the second, 'speech.'

6. 天气 **tiān-qi** — Hint: the first character means 'heaven,' and the second means 'spirit' or 'mood.'

7. 中国 **Zhōng-guó** — Hint: the first character means 'middle'; the second means 'country' or 'kingdom.'

Answer key

7. The 'middle kingdom' is China.
6. Heaven's mood equals the word for 'weather.'
5. Make speech electric, and you get the word 'telephone.'
4. Mountains and waters together mean 'landscape.'
3. A person's word means 'trust.'
2. A person leaning against a tree means 'to rest.'
1. A house with a woman in it means 'peace.'

Geography

Chinese geographical names (cities)

Peking	Běi-jīng
Shanghai	Shàng-hǎi
Tientsin	Tiān-jīn
Canton	Gǔang-dōng
Sian	Xī-ān
Taipei	Tái-běi
Hangchow	Háng-zhōu

Foreign countries

Canada	Jiā-ná-dà
India	Yìn-dù
Japan	Rì-běn
United States	Měi-guó
France	Fà-guó
Germany	Dé-guó
Italy	Yì-dà-lì
England	Yīng-guó

Useful addresses

United States Embassy (in Běi-jīng)
17 Guang-hua Lu,
Jian-guo-men-wai
General number: 52–2033

China Travel Service (head office) (Běi-jīng)
6 Dong Chang-an-jie
Tel: 55–4192

China Airlines (CAAC) (in Běi-jīng)
Ticket office
Zhu-shi Da-jie
Tel: 55–4415

Far Eastern Publications
Yale University
340 Edwards Street
New Haven, Connecticut 06520
Tel: (203) 436–1075
(for books and tapes on the Chinese language)

China Books and Periodicals
125 Fifth Avenue
New York, New York 10003
Tel: (212) 677–2650
(for books on the People's Republic of China)

Embassy of the People's Republic of China (New York City)
520 Twelfth Avenue
New York, New York 10036
Tel.: (212) 279–0885

Consulate General of the People's Republic of China
    (Washington, D.C.)
2300 Connecticut Avenue, N.W.
Washington, D.C. 20008
Tel. (202) 328–2500

Key to exercises and test

Chapter 1
1. Nǐ hǎo.
2. Wǒ hǎo, xiè-xie. Nǐ ne?
3. Wáng xiān-sheng, nín hǎo. Lǐ Fū-rén, nín hǎo. Máo nǚ-shì, nín hǎo.
4. Nín shì nǎ-guó rén?
5. Wǒ shì Měi-guo rén.
6. Nín guì-xìng?
7. Wáng xiān-sheng, nín hǎo.
8. Zhào xiān-sheng, nín hǎo.
9. Duì-bu-qǐ, duì-bu-qǐ!
10. Qǐng nín bāng-zhù wǒ. Xiè-xie. Zài-jiàn.

Chapter 2
1. Nǐ hǎo. Yǒu kòng fáng-jiān ma? Dān-rén-fáng. Sì-tiān. Duō-shao-kuài rén-mín-bì? Hǎo. Zhè shì wǒ-de hù-zhào.
2. a. 4 b. 1 c. 2 d. 5 e. 3
3. wǔ, shí, sān, èr, èr-shí, sì-shí, yī, liù, qī, jiǔ, wǔ-shí, sì, bā, sān-shí.
4. 834, 125, 578, 346, 879, 634.
5. Nín hǎo. Wǒ shì Měi-guo rén. Wǒ xìng Yuē-hàn-shēn. Zhāng xiān-sheng, nín hǎo.

Chapter 3
1. b.
2. b.
3. c.

4 b.
5 b.
6 c.
7 c.
8 sān-jiàn máo-yī. liù-ge dì-tú. liǎng-píng Zhōng-guó jiǔ.
9 jiǔ kuài qián. yí-kuài qián. wǔ-kuài qián. (total): shí-wǔ-
    kuài qián.
10 Nín hao. Yǒu méi-yǒu máo-yī? Bù-xǐ-huan. Yǒu bíe-de
    ma? Hen xǐ-huan. Duō-shao qián? Hǎo, wó mǎi. Xiè-xie,
    zài-jiàn.
11 Wǒ xiǎng mǎi máo-yī. Èr-shí-kuài qián. Wǒ yào sān-ge.
    Yǒu. Hěn hǎo-kàn. Wǒ hěn xiang mǎi. Wǒ yào liù-píng.
    Wǒ hen xǐ-huan. Méi-yǒu dì-tú.
12 b. b. b.

Chapter 4
1 1. a   2. c   3. b
2 Qǐng gěi wǒ cài-dān. yí-ge gōng-bǎo jī-dīng, yí-ge bái-cài
    dòu-fu. Liǎng-píng Qīng-dǎo pí-jiǔ. Hái yào liǎng-bēi
    shuǐ. Qǐng gěi wǒ zhàng-dān. Zhè shì sān-kuài qián. Xiè-
    xie, zài-jiàn.
3 a. Wǒ xiǎng chī hóng-shāo yú.
    b. Wǒ xiǎng chī Běi-jīng kǎo-yā.
    c. Wǒ xiǎng chī bái-cài dòu-fu.
    d. Wǒ xiǎng chī yí-ge gōng-bǎo jī-dīng.
4 a. Qǐng bāng-zhù wǒmen diǎn-cài.
    b. Qǐng gěi wǒmen Yīng-wén-de cài-dān.
    c. Qǐng kāi zhàng-dān.
    d. Qǐng jiāo wǒ zěmma yòng kuài-zì.
5 1. d   2. c   3. a   4. b   5. e
6 a. Nín hǎo.
    b. Wǒ xiǎng hē yì-bēi kā-fēi.
    c. Wáng xiān-sheng, zài-jiàn.
    d. wǔ-ge ren.
7 b.
8 b.
9 c.

Chapter 5
1 a. Fù-jìn yǒu méi-yǒu yóu-jú?
    b. Fù-jìn yǒu méi-yǒu yín-háng?
    c. Fù-jìn yǒu méi-yǒu gōng-yuán?
    d. Fù-jìn yǒu méi-yǒu fàn-guǎr?
    e. Fù-jìn yǒu méi-yǒu bǎi-huò dà-lóu?
2 Qǐng wèn, bó-wù-guan zémma zǒu? Qǐng nín màn yi-diǎn
    shuō. Xiè-xie, zài-jiàn.

3 Fù-jìn yǒu méi-yǒu Yóu-yì Shāng-diàn?
    a. Yes.
    b. First left, and then right.
    c. four streets.
4 1. c   2. a   3. c
5 a. Tīan-ān-mén, zémma zǒu?
    b. Left.
6 1. a   2. b   3. c
7 a. dào-le dì-èr-ge lù-kǒu, wàng zuǒ-biān zǒu, guò yì-tíao
    jīe, jiù (then) wàng yòu-biān zǒu, jiù kàn-jian-le.
    b. dào-le dì-èr-ge lù-kǒu, jiù kàn-jian-le.
    c. dào-le dì-yí-ge lù-kǒu, wàng yòu-biān zǒu, jiù kàn-jian-
    le.

Can you 'get by' test

1 a. Wáng xiān-sheng, nín hǎo.
    b. Lǐ nǔ-shì, nín hǎo.
    c. Zǎo.
    d. Zài-jiàn.
    e. Lǐ Fū-rén, nín zǎo.
2 a. Nín hǎo.
    b. Nǐ hǎo ma?
    c. Wǒ hěn hǎo. Xiè-xie. Nǐ ne?
3 1. e 2. a 3. d 4. j 5. b 6. h 7. i 8. c 9. f 10. g
4 a. qǐng gěi wǒ cài-dān.
    b. wǒmen yào sān-bēi pí-jiǔ.
    c. wǒmen yào liǎng-bēi chá.
    d. wǒmen yào yì-bēi kā-fēi.
    e. wǒmen yào yì-bēi shuǐ.
5 a. Wǒ xiǎng mǎi liǎng-píng Zhōng-guó jiǔ.
    b. Wǒ xiǎng mǎi Běi-jīng dì-tú.
    c. Wǒ xiǎng mǎi yí-jiàn máo-yī.
6 a. Bó-wù-guǎn zài nǎ-li?
    b. Tīan-ān-mén Guǎng-chǎng, zémma zǒu?
    c. Fù-jìn yǒu méi-yǒu fàn-guǎr?
    d. Yín-háng zài nǎ-li?
    e. Fù-jìn yǒu méi-yǒu yóu-jú?
    f. Bǎi-huò dà-lóu zài nǎ-li?
7 a. To the right.
    b. Go left at the corner.
    c. Go two blocks and you'll be there.
    d. At the first intersection, go right.
    e. After four blocks, go left; at the intersection, go
    right, and you'll see it.

8   a. two dollars.
     b. thirty cents.
     c. five cents.
     d. fifteen dollars.
     e. four dollars and twenty-five cents.
     f. one dollar eighty-five.
     g. fourteen dollars.

9   a. Wǒ xiǎng chī jī.
     b. Hěn xǐ-huan.
     c. Bù-yào hē kā-fēi.
     d. Liǎng-píng. Bù-xǐ huan.

10 a. Duō-shao qián?
     b. Wǒ mǎi zhèi-ge.
     c. Lǚ-guǎn zài na-li?
     d. Běi-jīng Fàn-diàn, zémma zǒu?
     e. Qǐng nín zài shuō.
     f. Wǒ xiǎng hē yì-bēi kā-fēi.
     g. Wǒ shì Měi-guo rén.
     h. Qǐng nín shuō Zhōng-guo huà.
     i. Yǒu méi-yǒu dì-tú?

Chinese-English word list

NB: All translations are as used in this book.

B

bā *eight*
-bǎi *(number unit for 'hundred')*
bái-cài *(Chinese) cabbage*
bái-cài dòu-fu *cabbage with bean curd*
bǎi-huò dà-lóu *department store*
bāng-zhù *to help*
bā-shí *eighty*
bā-yuè *August*
běi-fāng cài *northern style Chinese food*
Běi-jīng *Peking*
Běi-jīng dì-tú *map of Peking*
Běi-jīng Fàn-diàn *The Peking Hotel*
Běi-jīng kǎo-yā *Peking roast duck*
Běi-jīng cài *Peking style Chinese food*
bó-wù-guǎn *museum*
bù- *(negative prefix)*
bù-ké-yi *not OK, not all right*
Bù-láng *(transliteration for 'Brown')*
bú-xiè *you're welcome*
bù-xǐ-huan *don't like, don't care for, dislike*

C

cài *dish (of food, as in meat dish, chicken dish, etc.)*
cài-dān *menu*
cān-chē *dining car (on train)*
chá *tea*
chē *bus, vehicle (of any sort)*
chē-zhàn *train OR bus station*
chī *to eat*
chuáng *bed*
chū-kǒu *exit*
chūn-tiān *spring(time)*

D

dān-rén-fáng *single room*
dào-le lù-kǒu *when you get to the intersection*
Dà-rén *(name of Chinese person on tape)*
dà-shí-guǎn *embassy*
dǎ-suàn *plan to*
Dé-guó *Germany*
Dé-guó rén *German person*
diǎn-cài *to order food (in a restaurant)*
diàn-yǐng-yuàn *movie theater*
dì-èr *the second . . .*
dì-fāng *place, locality*
dì-sān *the third . . .*
dì-sì *the fourth . . .*
dì-tú *map*
dì-wǔ *the fifth . . .*
dì-yī *the first . . .*
dōng-tiān *winter*
dōu *all*
dòu-fu *bean curd*
duì-bu-qǐ *excuse me; I'm sorry, unfortunately*
duō-shao? *how much? how many?*
duō-shao qián? *how much money?*

E

èr *two*
èr-yuè *February*

F

Fà-guo *France*
Fà-guo rén *French person*
fáng-hào *room number*
fáng-hào duō-shao? *What's the room number?*
fáng-jiān *room*
fàn-guǎr *restaurant*
fēi-jī-chǎng *airport*

fēn *counter for cents*
fù-jìn *nearby*
fū-ren *Mrs.*
fú-wù-tái *service desk (in hotel)*
fú-wù-yuán *attendant (i.e., employee in hotel, restaurant, shop, etc.)*
fú-wù-yuán tóng-zhì *comrade assistant (term of address for restaurant, hotel, or shop employee)*
fú-zhuāng-diàn *clothing store*

G
Gāo *(surname)*
gěi *to give*
gōng-bǎo-jī-dīng *Gong-bao chicken (dish)*
gōng-gōng qì-chē *public bus*
gōng-gōng qì-chē zhàn *public bus station*
gōng-yì měi-shù shāng-diàn *handicrafts shop*
gōng-yuán *(public) park*
guǎng-chǎng *(city) square*
Guǎng-dōng *Canton (province of China)*
Guǎng-dōng cài *Cantonese style Chinese food*
guì-xìng *(honorable) surname*
guò *pass by*
guò sān-tiáo jiē *go (pass by) three blocks*
gǔ-wán-diàn *antique shop*

H
hǎi-guān *customs*
hái yào ... *also want ...*
hàn-sǎn *parasol*
hǎo *fine*
hǎo *be good*
hǎo bù-hǎo? *How will that be? How are you?*
hǎo-kàn *be pretty, attractive*
hē *to drink*

hěn *very*
hóng-shāo yú *red-cooked fish (dish)*
Huái-tè *(transliteration for 'White')*
huàn *to exchange, change*
huān-yíng *welcome*
hù-zhào *passport*

J
jǐ- *how many (ten or under)?*
jī *chicken*
-jiàn *(counter for clothing)*
jiāo *to teach*
jiē *street*
jǐ-ge? *how many?*
jǐng-tài-lán *cloisonné*
jīn-tiān *today*
jǐ-píng? *How many bottles?*
jǐ-tiān? *How many days?*
jiǔ *wine, liquor*
jiǔ *nine*
... jiù dào-le ... *and you'll get there*
jiǔ-shí *ninety*
jǐ-wèi a? *How many persons?*
jiǔ-yuè *September*

K
kā-fēi *coffee*
kāi *make out (as in 'make out a bill')*
kāi zhàng-dān *make out a bill*
kàn-jian *to see*
kàn-kàn *take a look at*
kéyǐ *fine, OK*
kéyǐ ma? *Is it OK?*
kéyǐ ... ma? *May we ...?*
kòng *empty*
-kuài *(counter for 'dollars')*
kuài-zi *chopsticks*

L
Lǐ *(surname)*
liǎng- *two (of something)*

liǎng-kuài qián   *two dollars*
liǎng-máo qián   *twenty cents*
líng   *zero*
líng-shì-guǎn   *consulate*
lín yù   *shower*
liù   *six*
liù-shí   *sixty*
liù-yuè   *June*
lù-kǒu   *intersection, corner*
lǚ-guǎn   *hotel*
lǚ-xíng zhī-piào   *traveler's check*

M

ma   *(end of sentence question word)*
Mǎ   *(surname)*
mǎi   *to buy*
màn   *be slow*
màn yi-diǎn shuō   *speak more slowly*
Máo   *(surname)*
-máo   *(counter for 'dimes')*
máo-bǐ   *Chinese brush pen*
Máo-tái jiǔ   *'Mao-tai' wine (for toasting)*
máo-yī   *sweater*
Měi-guo   *United States*
Měi-guo rén   *American (person)*
Měi-líng   *(name of Chinese girl on tape)*
méi-yǒu   *do not have*
méi-yǒu-le   *all gone, none left*
mǐ-fàn   *rice*

N

nán cè-suǒ   *men's rest room*
nán-fāng cài   *southern-style Chinese food*
nǎ-guó rén?   *which nationality?*
nǐ   *you (singular)*
nián   *year*
nǐ-de   *yours*
nǐmen   *you (plural)*

nín guì-xìng?   *What is your name? (polite)*
nǐ hǎo   *Hello! How do you do! Good day/morning/afternoon/evening!*
nǐ ne?   *And how about you?*
nín   *you (polite)*
nín hǎo   *hello*
nǚ cè-suǒ   *ladies' room*
nǚ-shì   *Miss (in People's Republic)*

P

pí-jiǔ   *beer*
-píng   *(counter for bottles)*

Q

qī   *seven*
-qiān   *(number unit for 'thousand')*
qián   *money*
qiān-míng   *sign (one's name)*
qǐng   *please*
Qīng-dǎo pí-jiǔ   *Qing-dao beer*
qǐng gěi wǒ . . .   *Please give me a . . .*
qǐng nǐ . . .   *Will you please . . .*
qǐng nín . . .   *Will you please . . .*
qǐng nín zài shuō.   *Please say it again.*
qǐng wèn . . .   *May I ask . . .*
qī-shí   *seventy*
qiū-tiān   *autumn*
qī-yuè   *July*
qù kàn   *go to see*

R

ràng   *let (someone . . .)*
ràng wǒ   *let me . . .*
rén   *person*
rén-mín-bì   *People's (Republic of China) currency*
ruǎn-xí   *'soft-seat' class (on Chinese trains)*

S

sān *three*
sān-máo qián *thirty cents*
sān-shí *thirty*
sān-xiān tāng *'three-vegetable' soup*
sān-yuè *March*
shémma *what?*
shémma yàngr-de fáng-jiān? *what kind of room?*
shí *ten*
shì *to be*
shí-èr-yuè *December*
shí-yī-yuè *November*
shí-yuè *October*
shì zhōng-xīn *city center*
shū *book*
shuāng-rén-fáng *double room*
shū-diàn *bookstore*
shuǐ *water*
shuō *to speak, say*
sì *four*
Sì-chuān cài *Szechuan style Chinese food*
sì-máo qián *forty cents*
Sī-mǐ-zī *(transliteration for Smith)*
sì-shí *forty*
sì-yuè *April*

T

tài-tai *Mrs. (used by Chinese to address foreign married females)*
tāng *soup*
tè-kuài-chē *express train*
-tiān *day*
Tiān-ān-mén Guǎng-chǎng *Tian-an-men Square*
-tiáo *(counter for streets)*
tóng-zhì *comrade*
tuō-xié *slippers*

W

wàng *go (toward)*
Wáng *(surname)*

wàng-qián zǒu *go straight ahead*
wàng yòu-biān zǒu *go right*
Wàn-lǐ Cháng-chéng *The Great Wall of China*
wǒ *I, me*
wǒ-de *my, mine*
wǒmen *we, us*
wǔ *five*
wǔ-kuài qián *five 'dollars'*
wǔ-máo qián *fifty cents*
wǔ-shí *fifty*
wǔ-yuè *May*

X

xiǎng *to desire to, want to*
xiǎo-jie *Miss (used by Chinese when addressing unmarried foreign females)*
xiān-sheng *Mr., sir*
xià-tiān *summer*
xiè-xie *thanks*
xiè-xie nǐ *thank you*
xǐ-huan *to like*
xìng *to be surnamed*
xíng-li *luggage, baggage*
xìng-rén dòu-fu *almond bean curd (dish)*
xīng-qī-yī *Monday (see list in reference section)*

Y

yā *duck*
yào *to want*
yào-diàn *pharmacy*
yě *also*
yī *one*
yī-bǎi *one hundred*
yī-bēi *a glass of . . .*
yī-ge *one (of something)*
yí-gòng *altogether (for sums)*
yǐ-jīng *already*
yī-jiǔ-bā-lǐng nián *1980*
yī-kuài qián *one 'dollar'*
Yí-lù-píng-ān! *Have a good trip!*

yī-máo qián   one 'dime,' ten 'cents'

yín-háng   bank

Yīng-wén   English (language)

Yīng-wén-de cài-dān   English menu

yī-qiān   one thousand

yī-yuè   January

yòng   to use

yǒu   to have

yòu-biān   (the) right (side)

yǒu bié-de ma?   Do you have others?

yóu-jú   post office

yǒu méi-yǒu . . .?   Have you any . . .? Is there a . . .?

Yǒu-yì Shāng-diàn Friendship Store

yú   fish

yúan   (formal term for 'dollar')

yù-dìng   to reserve

yù-dìng-le   (already) reserved

Yūe-hàn-shēn   (transliteration for Johnson)

Z

zài   be at, on, in

zài-jiàn   good-bye, so long, see you later

. . . zài nǎ-li?   Where is . . .?

zài shuō   say once again

zǎo!   Good morning! (before 10 A.M.)

zěmma   how

zěmma yòng   how to use

. . . zémma zǒu?   How do (I) get to . . .?

zhāng   counter word for bed

Zhāng   (surname)

zhàng-dān   bill, check (in a store, restaurant, etc.)

Zhào   (surname)

zhào-xiàng   to take photos

zhè   this (as subject)

zhèi-ge   this (one of something)

zhèi-jiàn   this (article of clothing)

Zhè jiù-shì.   Here it is. This is it.

Zhōng-guo   China

Zhōng-guo Guó-jì Lǚ-xíng-shè China International Travel Service

Zhōng-guo huà   Chinese language

Zhōng-guo rén   Chinese person

zhù   to live at, stay at, reside

zhū-bǎo-hé   jewel box

zhuō-zi   table

zǒu   go (walk)

zuǒ-biān   the left (side)

English-Chinese word list

A

a, one *yí-ge* or *yi* plus appropriate counter
again *zài* as in *zài shuō* 'say it again'
airport *fēi-jī-chǎng*
all *dōu* as in *dōu chī mǐ-fàn* 'rice for all'
already *yǐ-jīng*
also *yě*
also want *hái yào*
altogether (in sum total) *yí-gòng*
antique shop *gǔ-wán-diàn*
April *sì-yuè*
'attendant' (worker, employee in store, hotel, etc.) *fú-wù-yuán*
August *bá-yuè*
autumn *qiū-tiān*

B

baggage (luggage) *xíng-li*
bank *yín-háng*
(to) be *shì*
(to) be (well) *hǎo* 'I am well' *wó hǎo*
bean curd *dòu-fu*
bed *chuáng*
beer *pí-jiǔ*
bill (check) *zhàng-dān*
book *shū*
booked up (no rooms left) *méi-yǒu kòng-fáng-jiān-le*
bookstore *shū-diàn*
bottle (counter for) *-píng* a bottle of wine *yì-píng jiǔ*
bus *gōng-gōng qì-chē*
bus stop *gōng-gōng qì-chē zhàn*
(to) buy *mǎi*

C

cabbage (Chinese) *bái-cài*
can one . . .? . . . *kéyi ma?*
Cantonese style food *Guǎng-dōng cài*
center of town *shì zhōng-xīn*
(to) change (exchange) *huàn*
check (bill of fare) *zhàng-dān*
chicken *jī*
China *Zhōng-guo*
China (International) Travel Service *Zhōng-guo Guó-jì Lǚ-xíng-shè*
Chinese language *Zhōng-guo huà*
Chinese person *Zhōng-guo rén*
chopsticks *kuài-zi*
city center *shì zhōng-xīn*
cloisonné *jǐng-tài-lán*
clothing store *fú-zhuāng-diàn*
coffee *kā-fēi*
comrade *tóng-zhì*
consulate *lǐng-shì-guǎn*
corner *lù-kǒu*
(to) cost (what does it cost?) *duō-shao qián*
course (dish of food) *cài*
customs *hǎi-guān*

D

day *tiān*
December *shí-èr-yuè*
department store *bǎi-huò dà-lóu*
'dimes' (counter) *-máo*
dining car (on train) *cān-chē*
dish (of food, course) *cài*
'dollars' (counter) *-kuài*
'dollar' (formal term) *yúan*
don't mention it (you're welcome) *bú-xiè*
double room *shuāng-rén-fáng*
(to) drink *hē*
drugstore *yào-diàn*
duck *yā*

E

(to) eat *chī*
eight *bā*
eighteen *shí-bā*
eighty *bā-shí*
eleven *shí-yī*
embassy *dà-shǐ-guǎn*
empty (unoccupied) *kòng*
England *Yīng-guo*
English menu *Yīng-wén-de cài-dān*
English person *Yīng-guo rén*
exchange *huàn*
excuse me *duì-bu-qǐ*
exit *chū-kǒu*
express train *tè-kuài-chē*

F

February *èr-yuè*
fifteen *shí-wǔ*
fifth *dì-wǔ*
fifty *wǔ-shí*
fine *hǎo*
first *dì-yī*
fish *yú*
five *wǔ*
floor *-lóu*
    second floor *dì-èr-lóu*
forty *sì-shí*
four *sì*
fourteen *shí-sì*
fourth *dì-sì*
France *Fà-guo*
French person *Fà-guo-rén*
Friendship store *Yǒu-yì Shāng-diàn*

G

Germany *Dé-guo*
German person *Dé-guo rén*
(to) give *gěi*
(please) give me . . . *qǐng gěi wǒ . . .*
(a) glass of . . . *yì-bēi . . .*
(be) good (well) *hǎo*
good-bye *zài-jiàn*
good day *nín hǎo*

good evening *nín hǎo*
good morning *nín hǎo*
good-looking (attractive) *hǎo-kàn*
good night (good-bye) *zài-jiàn*
go straight ahead *wàng qián zǒu*
go to see *qù kàn*
go to the right *wàng yòu-bīan zǒu*
Great Wall of China *Wàn-lǐ Cháng-chéng*

H

handicrafts shop *gōng-yì měi-shù sháng-diàn*
(to) have *yǒu*
    do you have any . . .? *yǒu méi-yǒu . . .?*
Have a good trip! *yí-lù píng-ān!*
hello *nín hǎo*
(to) help *bāng-zhù*
(please) help me *qǐng nǐ bāng-zhù wǒ*
hotel *lǚ-guǎn*
how *zěmma*
    how to use *zěmma yòng*
how do I get to . . .? *. . . zémma zǒu?*
How are you? *Nǐ hǎo ma?*
How long are you staying? *Nǐ xiǎng zhù jǐ-tiān?*
how many? *duō-shao?*
how many (persons)? *jǐ-wèi a?*
how much (money)? *duō-shao (qián)?*
how much is it? *dūo-shao qián?*
hundred (number unit) *-bǎi*
    one hundred *yì-bǎi*

I

I *wǒ*
intersection *lù-kǒu*

is (am) *shì*
it ('this') *zhèi-ge*
how much is it? *Zhèi-ge dūo-shao qián?*

J
January *yī-yuè*
jewel box *zhū-bǎo-hé*
July *qī-yuè*
June *liù-yuè*

L
ladies' room *nǚ-cè-suǒ*
(young) lady *xiǎo-jie*
left *zuǒ-bian*
(go) left *wàng zuǒ-bian zǒu*
(to) like *xǐ-huan*
(do you) like it? *Nǐ xǐ-huan ma?*
(I) like it. *Wó xǐ-huan.*
(I would) like (to eat) . . . *wó xiǎng chī . . .*
live (stay at) *zhù*
(take a) look at *kàn-kàn*
luggage *xíng-li*

M
make out a bill *kāi zhàng-dān*
Mao-tai wine *Máo-tái jiǔ*
map *dì-tú*
March *sān-yuè*
May *wǔ-yuè*
May I ask . . .? *Qǐng wèn . . .?*
May we . . .? . . . *kéyi ma?*
me *wǒ*
men's room *nán-cè-suǒ*
menu *cài-dān*
Miss *nǚ-shì, xiǎo-jie*
Mister *xiān-sheng*
Monday *xīng-qī-yī*
money *qián*
(good) morning! (early, before 10 A.M.) *Zǎo!*
movie theatre *diàn-yǐng-yuàn*
Mr. *xiān-sheng*

Mrs. *Fū-ren*
museum *bó-wù-guǎn*
my *wǒ-de*

N
(What is your sur-)name? *Nín guì-xìng?*
(What is your) nationality? *Nín shì nǎ-guó rén?*
nearby *fù-jìn*
(negative prefix) *bù-, méi-*
nine *jiǔ*
nineteen *shì-jiǔ*
ninety *jiǔ-shí*
northern style Chinese food *běi-fāng cài*
November *shí-yī-yuè*
(room) number *fáng-hào*

O
October *shí-yuè*
OK *hǎo*
one *yī*
one (of something) *yí-ge*
one hundred *yì-bǎi*
order food *diǎn cài*

P
parasol *hàn-sǎn*
park *gōng-yuán*
passport *hù-zhào*
Peking *Běi-jīng*
Peking Hotel *Běi-jīng Fàn-diàn*
Peking roast duck *Běi-jīng kǎo-yā*
Peking style food *Bei-jīng cài*
People's (Republic) currency *rén-mín-bì*
pen (Chinese brush) *máo-bǐ*
person *rén*
pharmacy *yào-diàn*
(take) photographs *zhào-xiàng*
place *dì-fāng*
plan to *dǎ-suàn*

please (will you) *qǐng nǐ* . . .
please give me . . . *qǐng gěi wǒ* . . .
please say it again *qǐng nín zài shuō.*
pleased to meet you. *Nín hǎo.*
porter *fú-wù-yúan*
post office *yóu-jú*
pretty *hǎo-kàn*

Q

Qing-dao Beer *Qīng-dǎo pí-jiǔ*

R

red-cooked fish *hóng-shāo yú*
(to) reserve *yù-dìng*
restaurant *fàn-guǎr*
rice *mǐ-fàn*
right *yòu-biān*
room *fáng-jiān*
room number *fáng-hào*

S

say it again *qǐng nín zài shuō*
second *dì-èr*
(to) see *kàn-jiàn*
September *jiǔ-yuè*
service desk (in hotel) *fú-wù-tái*
seven *qī*
seventeen *shí-qī*
seventy *qī-shí*
shower *lín-yù*
sign (one's) name *qiān-míng*
single room *dān-rén-fáng*
six *liù*
sixteen *shí-liù*
sixty *liù-shí*
slippers *tuō-xíe*
(I'm) sorry *duì-bu-qǐ*
soup *tāng*
southern style Chinese food *nán-fāng cài*

speak more slowly *qǐng màn yī-diǎn shuō*
(to) speak, say *shuō*
spring (season) *chūn-tiān*
(city) square *gǔang-chǎng*
station (bus) *chē-zhàn*
   train station *hǔo-chē-zhàn*
street *jiē*
(counter for streets) *-tiáo*
summer *xià-tiān*
to be surnamed *xìng*
(honorable) surname *guì-xìng*
   'What's your (sur)name?'
   Nín guì-xìng?
sweater *máo-yī*
Szechuan style food *Sì-chuān cài*

T

table *zhuō-zi*
tea *chá*
teach *jiāo*
ten *shí*
Tian-an-men Square *Tīan-ān-mén gǔang-chǎng*
thanks *xiè-xie*
thank you *xiè-xie nǐ*
(that's) OK *Hǎo.*
(movie) theater *diàn-yǐng-yuàn*
there is *yǒu*
there are *yǒu*
(are) there (any). . . nearby? *fù-jìn yǒu-méi-yǒu . . .?*
third *dì-sān*
   third floor *dì-sān-lóu*
thirteen *shí-sān*
thirty *sān-shí*
this one *zhèi-ge*
this article (of clothing) *zhèi-jiàn*
This is it. *Zhè jiù-shì.*
(one) thousand *yì-qiān*
three *sān*
three-vegetable soup *sān-xiān tāng*

today *jīn-tiān*
toilet (men's) *nán cè-suǒ*
  (ladies) *nǚ cè-suǒ*
train *huǒ-chē*
train station *huǒ-chē-zhàn*
traveler's checks *lǚ-xíng-zhī-piào*
(Have a good) trip! *Yí-lù-píng-ān!*
twelve *shí-èr*
twenty *èr-shí*
two *èr*
two (of something) *liǎng-*

U
United States *Měi-guo*
use *yòng*

V
very *hěn*

W
(to) want *yào, xiǎng*
water *shuǐ*
welcome *huān-yíng*
(you're) welcome *bú-xiè*
what kind of? *shémma yàngr-de?*
where is . . .? *. . . zài nǎ-li?*
wine *jiǔ*
winter *dōng-tiān*

Y
year *nián*
you (singular) *nǐ, nín*
you (plural) *nǐ-men*
yours *nǐ-de*

Z
zero *líng*

Emergency situations

Words and phrases you may need in a hurry

You can hear how to pronounce these words and phrases at the end of Cassette 2, side 2

Get help quickly!	**Kùai zhǎo rén bāng-máng!**
Call the police!	**Jìao jǐng-chá!**
Get a doctor!	**Zhǎo yī-sheng!**
Careful!	**Dāng-xīn!**
Stop!	**Zhàn-zhù!**
Fire!	**Jiu hǔo!**
Danger!	**Wēi-xǐan!**
Hurry up!	**Kùai!**
Please speak English!	**Qǐng shūo Yīng-wén!**

ITINERARY

DATE	PLACE

ITINERARY

DATE	PLACE

EXPENSES			
DATE	AMT.	U.S.$	FOR:

EXPENSES

DATE	AMT.	U.S.$	FOR:

PURCHASES

ITEM _____

WHERE BOUGHT _____

GIFT FOR _____ COST _____ U.S.$ _____

ITEM _____

WHERE BOUGHT _____

GIFT FOR _____ COST _____ U.S.$ _____

ITEM _____

WHERE BOUGHT _____

GIFT FOR _____ COST _____ U.S.$ _____

ITEM _____

WHERE BOUGHT _____

GIFT FOR _____ COST _____ U.S.$ _____

ITEM _____

WHERE BOUGHT _____

GIFT FOR _____ COST _____ U.S.$ _____

ADDRESSES

NAME _____

ADDRESS _____

_____ PHONE _____

NAME _____

ADDRESS _____

_____ PHONE _____

NAME _____

ADDRESS _____

_____ PHONE _____

NAME _____

ADDRESS _____

_____ PHONE _____

NAME _____

ADDRESS _____

_____ PHONE _____

ADDRESSES

NAME _____

ADDRESS _____

_____ PHONE _____

NAME _____

ADDRESS _____

_____ PHONE _____

NAME _____

ADDRESS _____

_____ PHONE _____

NAME _____

ADDRESS _____

_____ PHONE _____

NAME _____

ADDRESS _____

_____ PHONE _____

TRAVEL DIARY

DATE_____

DATE_____

DATE_____

DATE_____

DATE_____

DATE_____

DATE_____